Inspire

Compiled by

Rhonda Culton

TABLE OF CONTENTS

January 2017

Carla Jo!

Girl... we've got stories to tell! And, they are stranger than fiction!

Thank you for standing by me and for loving me regardless of the circumstances. I cannot ever think of my life without you in it!

Throughout my mental health challenges, you've been a rock for me. I KNOW I would not have survived in Atlanta at all without your love. THANK YOU!!

You will forever be a true sister.

Love Always!
"J"
Tara Lynette.

How It All Got Started—Rhonda Culton

The Inspirational Book Project was definitely a 'God Idea.' I always wanted to organize a compilation project. God dropped the idea in my head and heart and I went for it. Originally, I was going to target a particular audience but God reminded me that everyone has a story. He wanted me to choose women who wanted to inspire others, encourage them, and share their story with the world. I began to search for women who had gone through tough times but refused to give up.

My personal mission is to encourage and inspire any and every one I come in contact with. For those of you that know me I am as transparent as transparent can be; this is just the nature of who I am. This is how God made me but I realize everyone is different. Many may not lay it all on the line or tell it all, but I was searching for those who wouldn't mind sharing their story.

The project started with over twenty women and ended with a committed and dedicated thirteen. For most of the women this would be their first time telling their story or writing like this. During conference calls I pushed them to move forward. It was an emotional time for some of the women but we were all there to comfort and inspire one other through the process. The encouraging words the ladies gave each other were astounding. We built a sister-bond that will never be broken.

The name of the book didn't come until mid-way through the project. I knew this was an inspirational project but I wasn't sure what God wanted me to name the book. As time progressed the name **INSPIRE** resonated in my spirit. *That's it!* I thought.

I am extremely proud of each of these powerful women. They became transparent in hopes of encouraging you. They share, in spite of their hardships, how they made it through. They share painful details of childhood molestation, rape, and violence because the trick of the enemy did not work: they made it and you will too. There is a light at the end of the tunnel so don't give up or give in. God will be with you to the end.

This is not the first book compilation project I participated in but it is the first I would spearhead and I am thankful for each of the women who participated. This journey would not have been nearly as amazing without each of them. I have witnessed firsthand how powerful it is to come together and present stories that will empower and inspire others.

I pray this book will inspire you to keep moving forward toward the destiny planned by God for your life.

Dedicated to you— The Inspirational Book Project presents: **Inspire,** *the book. Be Blessed.*

Inspire

Maelina Berry

Maelina Berry began surviving all odds at a young age. At nineteen she started her own business as a freelance multi-media producer, photographer and videographer. She has interviewed many gospel artists, movie producers, and actors. She is also the author of "I Have A Purpose."

Married at twenty-one, Maelina is a wife, homemaker and mother of two adorable energetic sons. When she isn't running around after her two loving boys she is spending time with her caring husband. She also blogs on her website "Lady Linas 411."

You can reach Maelina Berry by email at sohappygolucky18 @yahoo.com.

I HAVE A PURPOSE

by Maelina Berry

From what I've heard, mother was beautiful with warm brown eyes, amazing long flowing hair, cocoa brown skin, and very intellectual. Every mans dream girl. My father is a warm hearted with dark brown curly hair, dreamy brown eyes, with a smile as bright as the sun and one of the hardest working men I know. These two lovers met at church and later became middle school sweethearts. They eventually married and had three beautiful children.

It was Sunday morning, the sun was beaming, the birds chirping, two little toddlers were running around and I, a newborn baby, lay quietly in the playpen. After breakfast, got dressed and attended church as usual at St. Rest Missionary Baptist Church. After our morning church service, the members fellowshipped and ate together before heading out to an afternoon service. Back in the day it was pretty common to attend more than one church service on any given Sunday. The church we were going to attend not only invited the entire congregation, the also personally asked my mother to sing a solo.

My mother, older brother, oldest sister and I were headed to our "sister church." There were nine of us loaded into the 1989 four-door Nissan Sentra. We packed in. It was crowded but they made it work. A young driver was behind the wheel that day. My mother wanted to teach her how to drive. Many passengers were without seat belts and I was not in a car seat.

Before anyone in our car could react, the driver lost control, swerved into another lane causing our vehicle to be struck. My mother died on the scene and my siblings passed away at the hospital. I was the youngest survivor. I was only one month old. Each anniversary of the accident I try to shake the feeling and thought of why me. Why was I kept alive, Lord? Why would you allow my mother, brother and sister to die?

My grandparents raised me and my brother, who was four, for the first few years of my life. My grandfather is a very well rounded gentlemen who deserves a lot more credit than what he is given. My grandmother is a strong and caring woman who really loves her grandchildren dearly. They made sure that I was rooted in the Word of God as a young child. "Train up a child in the way he should go, and when he is old he will not depart from it." Proverbs 22:6 is a scripture I know they live by.

Growing up I was scared to ask questions but I was always curious about my mother. I always wondered what was she like as a child or young woman. I often would daydream about her being in the next room. It seemed so real. Now I cherish my oldest brother's fond memory of my mother singing to me as a newborn "Rock a bye baby."

During the time of my early childhood I remember my grandfather taking care of me and my brother. He worked the night shift which enabled him to be home in time to drop us off at school. Him walking us to school every morning and my grandmother picking us up afterwards is a dear memory for me. During summer vacation our grandfather took us on our annual road trip to Charlotte, North Carolina to visit family. We always had a blast.

As a young child I recall mostly seeing my father on Sunday. It made Sunday very special to me. From time to time I would spend the night at his house. It was nice to see him outside of church. I could feel my grandmother was not happy when I would leave for the weekend. It made me sad. I was so delighted to be spending time with my dad. I felt as though I had to choose sides. All the while I was stuck in the middle of the mess. All I wanted was peace. My grandfather was my happiness in the middle of it all. He made sure that I had a great childhood. We have so many special memories together: road trips, going to get an ice cream cones from Rite-Aid, Ragin' Waters and plenty of Bible Jeopardy.

One night my father met a young woman while attending our church revival. They exchanged numbers and began to talk. One fall day these two went out and realized they would like to further their relationship. Eventually, I started to tag along and enjoy some quality time with them. It felt good to have fun and feel like a family. I could tell my father was happy and that he found someone special.

They married February 4, 1998. I was still living with my grandparents and visiting my dad and bonus mom on the weekends. Tired of the back and forth, I wanted to move in with my dad. Eventually, I finally moved into my new home. I was happy and excited to start this new journey as a family. Sadly, my grandmother was not very happy about it. Didn't it matter where I wanted to live?

As a newly established family we continued to attend St. Rest on Sundays, which seemed to be uncomfortable for my dad and bonus mom. My cousins were attending the church too which made things just a little better. As time passed our season at the church ended. One day my family withdrew membership from St. Rest and began to attend church at Holy Living Community Church.

It was around this time a life changing event occurred in my life. A young man in my life that I trusted molested me. I can kind of recall the moment it all began. It was as if he had it out for me and only me. The abuse took place at his parents home somewhere I most definitely thought I was out of harm's way. He was someone in my life that I trusted so I thought what we were doing was normal. The abuse continued until I was in middle school. I remember when I overheard the news he would not be coming back. I was so happy. I often wondered why this had happened to me. Would this have happened if my mother was alive? I never told anyone because I was made to believe it was my fault.

I made up in my mind as a young woman I was not going to use my mother's tragic death or any circumstance as an excuse not to succeed. I knew that I had a purpose and I was determined to fulfill my God given assignment. I was not going to become bitter or angry.

Back in the day I could always count on my oldest brother to look after me. As a little sister I was constantly tagging along, asking him questions and wanting to do everything he did. He is the classic big brother always protecting me. Sadly, as time progressed I noticed a change in him. His attitude became more defiant and our relationship became more distant.

To this day, my loved ones are still coping with the passing of my family. Many can't shake the feeling of disbelief that they are gone. I'm not sure how my oldest brother coped with my mother's passing. All I know is that he is grieving in his own way.

It was always said that I got all the attention. In a sense this was true. I was the miracle baby saved from death in the car accident. I was often told things like, "Well, you didn't know her." At times, I have felt as though my feelings did not matter. Personally, I have coped in a very subtle manner. I have seen countless pictures and love letters I read for the first time when I was 17. I heard my mother's voice on a cassette tape. I have come to understand that my mothers mission on earth was complete and I was saved because I have a purpose.

For a short while it was uncomfortable at family events. As soon as I walked in everyone would stare at me and whisper. At a young age many family members said mean things to me like, "People are only nice to you because you look like your mother." The worst thing that was said to me was, "You're only a favorite because you survived the accident." I never let their comments make me angry, instead I smiled and walked away, something I learned from my father at an early age. Proverbs 19:11 "The discretion of a man deferreth his anger; and it is his glory to pass over a transgression."

Around the time of middle school I felt as though looking liking my mother was such a curse. I was this young girl with a beautiful heart, long hair, brown eyes and what they thought was a perfect life. All the guys loved my hair. They would come up to me and ask if they could touch it or ask "is it real?" There was this one girl in particular who was so jealous of my hair. She tried her best to get everyone to hate me. I eventually learned to thank God for my beauty and embrace my long hair. I will praise thee; for I am fearfully and wonderfully made: marvelous are thy works; and that my soul knoweth right well. Psalms

139:14

As time progressed, I graduated from High School, went to college, got married and had two beautiful kids. With everything that has happened in my life from my family passing in 1991 to my present life (2016), I still say that I am blessed with a purpose. One of my favorite books in the bible Ecclesiastes 3:1-8. *"To everything there is a season, and a time to every purpose under the heaven…"* Everything happens for a reason and a season.

As I am growing more in my spiritual life I am starting to realize my purpose. I have been blessed with the gift of dreams. The Lord gives me visions of events that will take place in the near future or in the long run. I plan to further my spiritual gifts and serve the Lord the best I can. "Now there are diversities of gifts, but the same Spirit. And there are differences of administrations, but the same Lord…" 1 Corinthians 12: 4-6

No one ask for a specific gift. You are blessed with it at birth. It is up to you to use your gift and fulfill the God designed purpose you were called to do. Use your gifts to honor God, encourage and strengthen others. "Every good gift and every perfect gift is from above," James 1:17

We have great challenges but with God's help, we will conquer them. Have faith and know God will not bring you to it if He would not bring you through it. God is all knowing, the Alpha and Omega, the beginning and the end.

Sometimes we look at other people's lives and wonder what life would be like in their shoes. Not realizing that the grass is not greener on the other side. Pray and believe in God's will for your life. Proverbs 19:21 "There are many devices in a man's heart; nevertheless the counsel of the LORD, that shall stand."

As a child of God we are commanded to forgive. While forgiving, learn to love those who wronged you. Just remember you have a purpose. Keep this word in your heart, "And we know that all things work together for good to them that love God, to them who are called according to his purpose." Romans 8:28.

Tosha Craft

Tosha Craft is a poet, writer, speaker, and educator who doesn't mind laying it all on the line as long it helps someone else. She has spent most of her years mentoring and inspiring others to push past their obstacles and be better. Teaching is her passion. Her primary purpose in life is to educate and empower in all she does by engaging people of diverse backgrounds, cultures and denominations. With her passionate personality, Tosha captivates her audiences by drawing them in with a personal, down-home approach. She is open and receptive, candid and compassionate, only asking for the listener to be open to the exchange.

Her story of success proves that it is not where one comes from but where one wants to go. Tosha is an overcomer. Despite life's many challenges, she is a graduate of Northeastern State University with a BA in English and went on to attain her M.Ed. at Langston University. Fully committed to the cause of motivating others, she is active in her community: fostering relationships with community organizations, providing scholarships for local seniors, and promoting community development. She is also the mother of three very active children: Elijah, AJanee, and Jayson; they are her primary ministry.

IN THE DARKEST CORNERS

(The Lamb Among Wolves)

by Tosha Craft

I had always been a serious child, and on most days, there was a nervousness around others that made me nauseous. It has never been clear where these feelings came from, but as a young girl, I often struggled with low self-esteem and a lack of confidence. These feelings began to intensify when my mother left my younger sister and me with our grandmother.

Our mother was moving to another city with the father of my youngest sibling. In reflection, I can understand her not wanting to involve us in the business of getting on with her life until she was sure. As a mother, I fully understand wanting to protect children from the intricate nuances of new relationships and sometimes established ones too. But this time was different from the others because she decided to take our youngest sibling; she was his child. In that decision, she had reinforced all the things I had believed to be true: that I was not good enough, that I was no more than insignificant, that I could not possibly be loved.

Abandonment is a powerfully debilitating and cankerous sore that festers and eats away at one from the inside. If not properly tended, the wound has the potential to ooze into other parts of one's life. For me, it was a further decline in my attitude. My emotions hovered between cloudy to torrential rains depending on the day, and I cried over the minutest of things. I cried because I missed my mother. I cried because my sister had more food on her plate. I cried because it was Tuesday. There was no rhyme or reason for it; it was just something I felt the need to do. At those times, I wanted my mother to love on me, to assure me that I was important, to show me that I mattered.

The year I entered middle school, my mother came to retrieve us. It was around this time that the first wolf entered my life; the wolf in sheep's clothing. He was older by three years, and I was a lamb for the slaughter. Completely naive, I was not prepared for the cunning wiles of boys or anything related to them. Besides a few elementary crushes and one or two furtive middle-school kisses, I had limited experience. It began innocent enough. Our first kiss broke open the brokenness in me, filling in the missing spaces. I was hooked. The first requests were school girl sweet: a kiss here, a gentle hug there. As time passed, they became more demanding and perverse. The fear of abandonment was so overwhelming, I complied.

Other girls spoke of their first time as if it was a wonderful experience, a transition into their womanhood.

For me, I blocked out my first experience as one would block the sun. I do not recall the taking of a young girl's most prized possession. I do not remember the breaking and tearing of gentle membranes. My most vivid memory of this time was when he had taken all that he could, he moved on anyway. I returned to square one, looking to fill the hole in my heart. A rosebud both opened and wilted at the same time, blooming too fast.

The following year, I spent the lazy summer afternoons learning to drive a stick shift and spending hours at the church. Whole summer days were easily consumed by Vacation Bible School, Baptist Training Union, choir rehearsals, musicals and the like. Commingled with what I felt was my family's desire to spend every waking moment between the church walls, I was also transitioning. Like the gentle washing of the baptismal, I was coming into myself that summer. Bony arms and legs began to soften and round. I was young, supple, and dare I say, womanly. It was around this time that a particular deacon took an interest in me. I would often encounter him on my way about the city. As we passed, we would exchange a wave here or have a casual conversation as he mowed his impeccable lawn. Young and trusting, I thought nothing of it. He was, after all, a respected member of our community: a family man, a father, and very active in the church. My family trusted him, so I had no reason not to.

When he began to invite me into the house that summer, I thought nothing of it. These solo visits were harmless enough in the beginning, an offering of a cool drink. They progressed into hour long conversations, the likes of which I cannot recall, but could not have been much deeper than a toddler's wadding pool. When he began to rub my bare leg, I did not flinch. When that progressed to him kissing me coyly on the lips, still I did not falter. The day he took me to the bed he shared with his wife, I was shaking. He assured me that it was normal for me to be nervous and promised to be gentle. He did not mind the blood or the brokenness; he cleaned me up and sent me out the door as if nothing had ever taken place. The next Sunday, there he was, wolf among the flock, hiding in plain sight.

I have never spoken of this incident until now. For many years, I shielded and protected this man, more than twice my age, because somehow I felt it must have been my fault. At that time, I did not know the word: Pedophile. Crimes against the young were always whispered in hushed tones, and "what happened in the house stayed in the house." I know better now. But at the time, I felt there was no one I could pour my secrets into. In the years following, there were several similar incidents. None of which I shared or even talked about. I held them grave deep, etched inside my heart, each breach further validating the belief that it had to be my fault. I accepted that this was how life was supposed to be and behaved accordingly. I grew secretive and quiet.

The summer of my eighteenth year, I fully embraced my independence by moving in with a few friends. We were young and wild and carefree. One night or rather early morning, we had gone to visit a guy one of the girls dated. On this particular night there were several new faces. One of which was a young male with a gravelly voice. For reasons only known to him, the raspy voiced man ordered several girls to attack us. I was a tiny thing back then, but I fought until my hands were bloody. When he barked that I would be "the hood toy," my only instinct was to flee. There was no doubt about his meaning; his plan was to serve me like some lamb to the slaughter. I bolted, praying that my sprinter's legs could carry me to shelter and protection less than two or three city blocks away.

He caught me easily less than a block from my destination. My legs had not been as fast as the BMX he was peddling. Hopping off the bike, he commanded that I go back with him. Going back to the wolf's den was not an option. With one blow, the Big Bad Wolf caused my face to crumble, left a bloody gash across tender lips, as he dragged me up the driveway of a nearby house. Secluded by the sleeping cars and the cover of crepuscular darkness, he bent me over a rusty hood, tore off clothing, and forced his way in between desert dry spaces. After he finished, he still wished to take me back with him. The instant he turned his back, I shot in the opposite direction.

The police were called. Questions were asked, so many questions. There was a silent ride to a very cold hospital. A rape kit determined that I had indeed been raped. Pictures were taken. In them, I resembled a boxer who had lost very badly. A scalding shower washed his scent from my skin. Pain medication was given. I wished to sleep indefinitely. Rooms remained dark for several weeks until I could heal physically. A scar formed on my upper lip as a reminder. I became a volcano on the verge of eruption. He was found. A court case ensued. I was sent out into the world angry but also strangely empowered.

Prior to this incident, I had at least known my assailants, and although that makes no difference, somehow I had categorized those exchanges as different. I could not rationalize or explain this latest injury. What gave him that right? Their must have been a reason I had been chosen. Why I had always been chosen? I must have been flawed in some way. My desire became to kill whatever weakness I possessed. I hardened my heart and vowed no one would ever prey on me again. I decided if I was going to continually lie down with wolves, I would behave like one, a she-wolf, dating who I wanted, sleping with who I wanted. I did anything I was big and bad enough to do. Sex satisfied some deep well in my belly that needed to be filled. I craved it, was in search of it, to be honest, it is a desire I have to fight daily. Like alcoholics to a bottle, this was my addiction. I fed my flesh and paid no mind to my soul. Flying high in the invincibility of youth, I gave no thought to what bottom looked like for me. What I eventually came to know was that the old, familiar emptiness that I felt could never be filled by man, and bound in my addiction, I desperately needed an intervention.

Rehab began when I came into the full knowledge that this problem could not be fixed in the way I had grown accustomed. Acceptance of ones faults is often difficult to do. We lie and trick ourselves into thinking that we must keep those things secret lest we be judged. The reality is that if we do not expose our inner most secrets, they often eat away at us like cancer. We are not weak because we have flaws. We succumb to weakness the moment we allow those hidden things to keep us bound.

1 John 1:19 says, "If we confess our sins, he is faithful and just to forgive us our sins, and to cleanse us from all unrighteousness." I began to confess all the thoughts and deeds that had me shackled. I laid my burdens down at His feet and asked him to have His way. In doing so, I learned that when we are at our lowest point, He gives us the power to persevere. For me, it was a move to a new state, a distancing from the people I associated myself with, and an opportunity to begin anew. For you, the process may be different, but the results will be the same. He will

elevate you from your valleys when you give Him a chance.

The next step to healing was forgiveness. So many people hold on to past hurts and pains, often hindering themselves when the perpetrator has long since forgotten. What does it profit us for the Father to forgive and we are still holding on? True forgiveness has very little to do with the wrongdoer and everything to do with becoming free.

Oh, how I wanted to be free. I had to tread some dark territory to forgive, unearthed traumas that were long buried. My desire was to forgive wholeheartedly and without regret, even when the offender denied there was ever an offense. This is no charge for the faint of heart. Forgiveness is often difficult and one-sided. Hate and bitterness are more simplistic; they are raw and unfiltered. But to heal, forgiveness is necessary. Forgive the people that have caused you pain and especially, forgive yourself. The latter is the most difficult because guilt hides in the furthest corners of our minds, and has the ability to reappear at the most inopportune times, taunting us like a schoolyard bully. But guilt has no power unless we give ourselves over to it. Do not replay the pain, do not meditate on negative thoughts, and do not think yourself less because of your experiences. Begin to see yourself how God sees you. You are beautiful, you are strong, you are worthy, you are loved, and you are victorious! Stand tall and know that you are even more priceless because you made it through.

No one makes it through alone. Had it not been for those who pushed and propelled me to keep going, I cannot imagine where I would be. Even when there was no desire to make it, there was always someone who spoke a word of life in my spirit. I have heard people boast about how independent they are as if their accomplishments are solely of their own making. This type of bravado is false and misleading. We all need a village, people who love us despite our shortcomings and our faults, shoulders to cry on and ears to listen. To believe otherwise is a dangerous and costly illusion. It is to our advantage to surround ourselves with people who will push us to our greatness and to uncover the hidden gems we have yet to discover about ourselves. My village provides care and safety. I have learned to be mindful and introspective when allowing others into its sacredness. This is imperative because if we allow the wrong people in our space it can impede our growth. Like-minded individuals gravitate toward each other. You cannot surround yourself with negative people and get positive results. It is also difficult to heal if the people in your circle are wounded and lack the desire to be mended. Examine your atmosphere. Are there people who are only taking up space? Are there haters and dissenters? Those people may be the ones hindering your wellness. Letting go of the dead things in our lives allows us to flourish and grow and to find peace even in the midst of our war. For the same reason we go to hospitals and not cemeteries to get well. A diseased relationship can impede your life and snuff out progress.

Everything shifts. Seasons change. Life begins and ends. I have found this to be my testimony: God can and will protect you and cause you to be victorious even when the enemy comes to take your life. There are people who need to know that they can progress from victim to victorious by shifting their paradigm. Letting go of people who mean you no good can be difficult, but there is great reward in helping someone who needs your particular testimony as an overcomer. The life you have lived makes you an expert of your experience, and each experience allows us to empathize with others who share similar stories.

As humans, we are charged with the exceptional duty of caring for others in need. I truly believe that is why the human spirit is both so fragile and resilient. It allows us to experience unbearable pain and then to heal with that same pain. Throughout the years, I have been able to share with a few my story and become a fabric of healing in theirs. I believe the catalyst for opening these wounds at this point in my life is to effect change, for me, for my children, for my students, and for anyone who is struggling with the isolation this type of trauma can cause. Know this: there are others among you who know. We have grown bold and vocal, and we will not stand silently by while you suffer. It is not your fault that these things happened to you. You do not have to hide the pain. Crack it in jagged pieces like shards of glass and share what you can to help someone else, healing yourself in the process.

There are times in our lives that bring tremendous sorrow, but it can and will get better when we do not give in to the bitterness of life. We are overcomers because of and despite our testimonies. When life has left us broken, we can rebound and win. Broken glass is still glass. It may not be possible to assemble it the same way, but if you try it by fire, it can become new. This even applies to us. 2 Corinthians 5:17 tells us when we come to Christ we become new and the things of our past are passed away. I have never been a stranger to prayer. I prayed often even while in the midst of my storm. Spending time in His presence God has kept me. Pray, meditate, and affirm good things over your life. Prayer can transform us and destroy yokes. When the lamb goes to the Shepherd, He can and will begin to pull out the things that do not resemble Him. I stand free today because whom the son sets free, is free indeed.

Barbara Mays

Barbara Mays has a passionate heart to do the will of God. You will always find her about her Father's business. She is dedicated to Kingdom building and spreading the word of God. God has given her so many talents. She is an interior designer, hair dresser, party and wedding planner. She will turn any event into a spectacular occasion. She is known as the "Diva of Style and Fashion."

Barbara Mays has been a Christian over twenty years with a fervent, heart to do the will of God. She enjoys helping the church and the church members. She is humble and never needs to be seen. She is a dedicated mother, wife and servant of God. Barbara has the spiritual gifts of casting out demons and is also a prayer warrior. She loves to make a change wherever she goes. For booking information, Barbara can be reached at: divabillions@gmail.com.

WHEN YOU'VE DONE ALL YOU CAN—JUST STAND

by Barbara Mays

I was a little girl living in Mississippi. At the age of nine, my father and another member of my family started molesting me. I suffered through this tragedy until I was fourteen years old. Because of the molestation, it was very difficult for me to trust men. I felt that men had failed me. On the inside, I hated them. I thought that I would never let any man touch me in any way. I even began to think that I could never be married, or have a healthy relationship with a man. Unfortunately, my molestation had the opposite effect. I began to allow men in my life that used me and abused me.

You are probably asking yourself, "How was it that her mother was not aware of her being molested by her father and another family member?" Well, I will tell you how this happened to me. My Dad worked in the evening. My Mom worked in the morning. She had two jobs that kept her away from home and from my nine siblings and me most of the time. It was during her long periods of working those two jobs that my father would molest me. In my heart, I believe that he arranged for it to be that way.

I can recall the first time that my father molested me. My mom was at work. My sisters and I slept in one room. As I was drifting off to sleep, my Dad opened our door and softly called my name. He said, "Come here Barbara. I want to show you something." My sisters were sound asleep. Obeying my Dad, I got out of my bed and went to him. He took my hand. I asked him "where are we going Daddy?" He said, "Just follow me." We went through the living room, to the kitchen, directly to the basement door. I asked him, "Why are we going in the basement daddy?" He said, "I have something to show you baby. Don't be afraid." He opened the basement door. It was dark down there. I became afraid. The basement had always been a room in our house that I hated. He led me down the stairs, and pulled the white light string that hung from the ceiling. He picked me up, and laid me on the laundry table where Mom would fold the clothes. I was afraid and confused! "Daddy!" I said. "I thought you had something to show me?" He placed his hand over my mouth and told me to shut up and be quiet. He said, "I do have something to show you. I will not hurt you. Just be still, and let Daddy show you how much he loves you."

He pulled down my panties, and proceeded to penetrate and molest me. The pain burned through me like a hot, sharp knife! The time seemed to stand still as my young mind thought, "When will he stop? When will he let me go?" I wanted to scream out for help, but my lips were frozen. After he was finished, he made me swear that I would not tell my Mom or anyone else. I did not tell her until I was fourteen years old.

Life was hard for us in Mississippi. Despite the fact that both my parents had jobs, it seemed that we were always struggling financially. There were nine of us children. My parents were never able to "make ends meet." Many times, we did not have enough food to eat. When things got very hard, my Mom would have to take us to a relative's house to eat. I remember how she would be so embarrassed. They would ask her "Where is your husband?" Mom even tried to get food stamps, but they said that she made too much money. We were starving! We were poor! We could not pay our bills, and they said that she made too much money!

Not only were we struggling to get food, my siblings and I traded our hand-me-down clothes and shoes with one another. We never had anything new. There were times when our neighbors would give us their kids' old clothes, but that did not make anything better for us. Life was so hard on us at that time. Many times, we went without light and gas. I do not know how my Mom managed, but now I understand that it was God's grace that was with her.

To make matters worse, my parents argued and fought constantly. They were always at each other's throats. My Dad was angry about his life. He seemed to be angry all of the time. Sometimes he would viciously beat my mother as we stood by terrified, helpless and unable to help her. Despite his horrible treatment of her, she stayed with him. She once told me that she did it to keep her family together. He continued to molest me in the basement and I never said a word.

When I was around thirteen years old, my parents decided to leave Mississippi. They were seeking a better life for our family. We moved to Cleveland, Ohio. I was so excited about moving to Cleveland. For me, the move represented a new beginning for me. At least, that is what I thought. The molestation stopped for a while. I believe it stopped because there was no basement for him to commit his heinous acts against me. I tried to hide my feelings about my father molesting me. I filed them in the back of my mind. It was in a place of darkness where I could not see or think about them anymore. Then, he started molesting me again. He started forcing himself on me when I was in the bathroom or when no one else was at home. Again, I was too terrified to scream or shout for help. This went on for another year.

By the time I turned fourteen, I got enough courage to tell my Mom that my father had been molesting me. After telling my Mom, I was relieved to know that she did not blame me. She believed me. She was sorry for what my Dad had done to me. That night she confronted him about the molestation. He called me a liar and a little whore! He swore that he had never touched me like that! He asked my mother, "How can you believe her? She must be crazy!" My mother told him that she believed me. When she said that, he slapped her in the mouth so hard that she fell on the floor! Blood was all over her face and on her white work shirt. He began to kick her and beat her uncontrollably! She tried to fight him back, but he overpowered her. I ran over to the neighbor's house to call the police. That night, he went to jail. We never saw him again. Without my father in the picture, my mother fell into financial hardship.

Our next-door neighbor, James, would always try to help us out as much as he could. James was a very kind young man who lived alone. His kindness was quite unusual for someone his age. He was always willing to help my mother. Whenever she was short on a bill, or on food, he was right there helping her keep her head above water. I fell in love with him. I never thought that true love would happen for me.

James and I had our first child, a girl, when I was eighteen. I felt like I had met the man of my dreams. He was, sweet, kind, and thoughtful. He loved our child. He was very good with her. In spite of what my Dad had done to me, I desired a healthy relationship with a man. This man had captured my heart and my soul. I wanted to be his wife, but we did not get married. Still, our relationship felt good. I felt that he loved me, and I loved him in return.

When I was twenty, we had a second child, a boy. Then, one day, I found out that he was cheating on me with my best friend. It felt as if he had taken a knife and plunged it into my chest! Once again, a man that I trusted wounded me. I asked myself, "How could he do this to me? After all, I had just brought our son into the world"! I had come to trust and believe in him. I felt betrayed. My whole world, once again, turned upside down! His lies and deceitfulness made me want to go back to where I started from; a place of not trusting men again. The trust that I had for him had been violated. I thought that my distrust for men had healed. This situation with James showed me that my molestation had left a gaping hole in my heart, spirit, soul, and mind. My mind told me that I would never heal. Eventually, James and I separated. I was alone with our two children. I went into a deep depression.

Time passed. James and I got back together in spite of the fact that I knew that he had not changed. When the baby was fifteen months old, I found out that I was pregnant again with my third child. I was confused. I just did not know what to do about my situation. I desperately needed to get myself together. I felt like I did not have anywhere to go. My mind told me that I would never heal. Instead of turning to a counselor, a pastor, or a trusted relative for guidance, I started going to clubs to party. I was mistakenly thinking that having more fun would erase my pain. Things only got worse.

One night, I went to a dance club alone. I met a man there. We danced, and had a good time. After partying with him a little longer, I told him that I was leaving. He asked if he could call me later. I gave him my number.

As I was leaving the club, I walked alone through the dark parking lot to find my car. As I was walking, I heard someone come running up behind me. With one swift move, he grabbed me by the neck! He had a knife! He put the cold, sharp edge of the knife to my throat. He told me that he was going to rape me! I was terrified! I could not fight back! I kept crying that I was pregnant! I cried and begged him to let me go! Glory be to God! My assailant let me go! Suddenly, he snatched me around facing him. The last thing that I wanted to do was look at him. Total shock and surprise seized me! I looked right into the eyes of the man that I had partied with and gave my number to! That terrible experience sent me into an even very deeper depression. I had a nervous breakdown.

After the rape, James and I left Cleveland with our children to try to make a new start on life. We moved to California. When I moved to California, I really thought things would get better. James and I were still not married. Life seemed to get worse for me.

At the age of two, my healthy baby girl developed meningitis. This was a devastating blow to my family. Meningitis had left her deaf. She stopped talking because she could not hear. To make matters worse, she had a stroke on her left side, which made her have to learn how to walk again. I thought that my family would step up and help us, but they just made matters worse.

Instead of embracing her, and helping her to feel normal, they treated her like being deaf was a disease. I had family members who were so insensitive that they would say to me, "What is wrong with her? She is just an embarrassment." For the most part, I kept my baby girl away from my family members. I never thought that my family could hurt my children and me so badly.

Everything bad seemed to be happening to me, something had to change. My sister invited me to a church service. I still thought to myself, what can that church do for me? I didn't want to have anything to do with the church. My sister continued to share about the love of Jesus and I decided to go to church with her. On April 23, 1988, I gave my life to Jesus Christ. That was when I started looking for Jesus instead of fun in the clubs. God found me! He saved me! I accepted Jesus Christ as my Lord and Savior! I knew that I would never be the same.

After I gave my life to the Lord, things didn't change right away. My mother had gotten sick and soon passed. Before her passing, taking care of her proved to be a daunting task. My daughter's sickness seemed to get worse. She was diagnosed with Type 1 diabetes. She was in the hospital for two long weeks.

One evening, while I was at the hospital with my sick child, I went to the chapel to pray. As I was praying, the Holy Spirit spoke to me and said, "If you leave him, a curse will be on you because you are the only Bible that he will read at this time. I want you to live like Jesus Christ in front of him, so he can see Jesus in you." I asked God, "Why do I need to stay with this man when he has hurt me so much? We are unequally yoked anyway!" Then God spoke to me again. He told me that He was going to save my husband and that I should just show the light that was on my life and he would draw my husband unto him. Then the Lord spoke His word from John 12: 32, "And if I, be lifted up from the earth, I would draw all men unto me." I obeyed the voice of the Lord, and stayed with my husband despite his unfaithfulness.

I began to pray for him. I recalled the passage of scripture from Ezekiel 37:1-3, as I was praying for him, the Lord said that it was my husband's last chance, and that he needed to accept Him as his Lord and savior. When I prayed that over him, tears rolled down his face and he stated that God was real. That was the beginning of his new life. He was still dealing with some life changing issues. Nevertheless, I stood on my faith in God. I truly believed that He would change my husband.

In spite of my anguish, I knew that this was a time where my faith in God had to be strong! There was no room for doubt! There was no room for fear! There was no giving up! There was only room for faith in the time of my storm! I had to take a stand for my daughter's sake no matter how I felt, or what I saw! Ephesians 6:11 says, "Put on all of God's armor so that you will be able to stand firm against all strategies of the devil." I had to stand on the word of God! I had to walk by faith and not by sight!

God gave my daughter nine more years of life. Before she passed away, she broke both of her hips and her left shoulder. She was almost totally blind. As I sat by her bedside one night, she told me that she was tired. I told her not to give up! Truth is that I knew in my heart that her time was nearer than I wanted it to be. As her mother, I was not ready to let her go. I prayed to the Lord. I told Him that I did not want to be selfish, but I did not want see my child die. Nonetheless, I was able to say, "Lord not my will, but your will be done."

My daughter took her last breath on February 25, 2016. Her last words were, "Lord Jesus Help Me!" She fought a good fight of faith. She had suffered for nine years, yet still believing for her healing until the end.

Are you willing to stand? Stand when you, or someone you know, have been sexually molested or raped? Are you willing to stand when you have an adulterous mate? Are you willing to stand when you're homeless and hungry? Are you willing to stand when your family kicks you to the curb? Are you willing to stand when the enemy is doing all he can to break you down? Remember this, Put on all of God's armor so that you will be able to stand firm against all strategies of the devil, Ephesians 6:11-13. If my God has done it for me, I trust and believe that He can do it for you. Don't give up. Trust in the Lord with all your heart, lean not to your own understanding. In all your ways acknowledge Him and He will direct your path, Proverbs 3:5. God has his hands on you. Can you count it all joy when you go through trials and tribulations? God will never leave you and God will not give you more than you can bare. Just give it to the Lord. When you have done all you can do, Just Stand.

Chanee A. Pruett-Anderson

Chanee was born on November 28, 1976, in Philadelphia, Pa. to a strong mother and a strong-willed father. Her parents divorced when she was 5 years old. Like many other children raised in a single parent household in the inner city, she was destined to rise above her circumstances. It wouldn't be an easy journey. Her story is filled with abandonment, rejection, depression, loss, isolation and fear. She is inspirational because she is a living testimony through her triumphs and defeats over obstacles that in some cases stifle many others. Chanee's story will motivate and cultivate the warrior spirit within us to keep fighting to survive and to obtain your successes in life.

Chanee A. Pruett-Anderson is a Graduate of California State University, San Bernardino with a BA in Biology. She is also an MBA student at California Baptist University. In addition, Chanee works as a Real Estate Professional, Travel Expert, and Owner of Chanee Says, which is a Life & Style brand. As a mother of three and stepparent to two, Chanee has vast knowledge and expertise in the areas of homemaking and utilization of resources. Women and Children in Transition was birthed from her own testimony in her time of need. This foundation will serve families that seek mentorship, food and shelter, mental health resources, educational guidance, networking and other areas of need.

For booking information, you can reach Chanee at chaneeanderson.inteletravel.com or chaneesays@gmail.com.

TURN YOUR PAIN INTO POWER

by Chanee A. Pruett-Anderson

I thought I was the perfect wife with the perfect husband living the "American Dream." Those overzealous expectations may have started years ago. As I reflect on my childhood and possibly where I conceived such notions, I have to start from the beginning.

I used to go to my grandmother's house just before school. I can recall eating buttered white toast sitting in a white plastic covered chair in her living room. As silly as it may sound, I used to like to watch the Jetsons in the morning. The opening theme song for The Jetsons starts with the whole family in the space car. Elroy is first to be dropped off at elementary school, Judy is next dropped off at the high school, and Jane is offered some cash to go shopping; rather she takes the whole wallet and is dropped off at the mall, all while George is driving. He is represented as the man and head of the house. For me, it sort of set the expectation that the man is supposed to go to work, while my responsibility was to care for the kids and spend my free time at the mall. Isn't this the ideal life? The Jetsons subconsciously represented the life I wanted to live. That life was quite different from my actual life being raised by a single mother in the inner city. It would have been nice to have a reference such as my own father for what life was supposed to be like rather than a cartoon. My reality simply wasn't like the representations of what I saw on tv.

At the end of the cartoon, George comes home, met by the housekeeper taking his briefcase. Then each family member greets him one by one with his chair, slippers, pipe, and a loving kiss by Jane. Astro then pulls George off to take him for a walk on the treadmill. Ironically, a cat disrupts the walk George and Astro are having, causing the treadmill to speed out of control. Don't we all remember this at the end? What's really interesting is that, while the treadmill is out of control, George screams, "Jane stop this crazy thing!" Is George, insinuating, that Jane is the root cause of the chaos in George's life? George is literally, going around and around on the out of control treadmill. George is looking for Jane to fix the problem. Isn't that what most women want? To be needed, not to be overworked or overstressed and to remedy the problems of life. Not to be blamed for mishaps or the hardships in life.

You might be asking yourself, why are we talking about this cartoon. In reality, most of our lives can be compared to that lifestyle whether it is similar or opposite of the images that are portrayed. I believe I knew from a very young age the type of life I wanted to live. I knew that I wanted to be married with kids. I'm not sure if it was in rebellion to the fact that my mother was happily divorced and I am an only child. Being an only child is a large contributing factor in how I have dealt with many issues in my life: Good and bad. When we really think about it, most of the problems that we are confronted with as adults stem from our childhood. While we think, we may have had a great childhood or not, we can get to the root causes of what pains us. Then we can begin to find solutions by examining our past and healing our present.

Four months into the pregnancy with my first child, I was told on the day that I was supposed to find out the gender of my child, that I had to remain on bed rest for the duration of the pregnancy in order for him to survive. How did a routine appointment turn into strict orders? I wasn't prepared, he wasn't prepared, and that is when the troubles began.

I had a good job, brand new car, and an apartment in one of the most affluent communities in California. As far as I was concerned I was doing well. I didn't have a dime saved in order to sustain my lifestyle. What was I supposed to do? The real question was, what were we supposed to do. I had to pay rent, car payments, and was expecting a brand new baby. Oh, and not to mention I was planning a wedding. Things got real at this point. The love I had for my future husband had very little to do with what I needed him to do as a man. I would say, this is where the breakdown in respect trust and communication started. Most black women have been raised by strong mothers, aunts and grandmothers. We have witnessed these women in our lives doing what they had to do to make things happen. But even, strong women need support. When I was told, I could no longer work, my expectation was that the man I was going to soon marry, could handle the responsibilities. Isn't this what George would have done? Rather than him stepping up when I was down, he didn't have the ability to do what was necessary at that time. The writing was on the wall and I chose to ignore the signs. To be truthful, I ignored the signs because I wanted my child to have a father in the home and I ultimately wanted to be married to the father of my child. I was told by my aunt, that just because we had a child, I didn't have to marry him.

At that time, I had bigger issues I was confronted with. My health and the health of my unborn child were at stake. It was a difficult time for both me and my son. The last few months of the pregnancy became consumed with doctor's appointments and hospital admittance that caused me to fear for our lives. This was the first time I had to consider life and death. Somehow I was courageous and faithful that my son and I would live. There were many days I lay in bed and simply prayed and spoke life into my unborn child. It was then that we formed our first bond. We were in it together, the fight for life. I had to receive steroid injections to speed up my son's development in case he was born premature. I had toxemia and many bouts of elevated blood pressure. By the time I delivered by son, my organs were shutting down. I was a very sick young woman with a healthy baby boy. I wasn't sure if I was going to survive.

I had some thoughts that perhaps my past was catching up to my present. I wasn't living right. I had three abortions prior to the conception of my first child. Was God punishing me? Those were my thoughts. I felt like God was saying to me, you can't play God and choose when you're ready to become a mother. I had chosen not to go forward with the other pregnancies and now that I was ready, this was happening to me. I had so much anxiety about my health and how to care for my newborn child. I found the strength and courage with support to manage my health and do what I needed to as a mother. That time passed so fast. At that point I had no idea if I could have had any more children. As an only child, I didn't want my son to be alone. That was a concern of mine stemming from my own childhood. I didn't really like being alone.

When I think I about it, in my adult life in dating, I have really never been alone. I can recall having boyfriends at a very young age. Literally from elementary all through college, not many of those years did I spend alone. Does this have anything to do with my present? It's very likely that fear of being alone or being alone can cause us to make choices in our lives that can be detrimental to our future self. It is healthy to be alone for a period of time. Especially while growing and maturing. It's not necessary to fill that void with a man rather than adventures and hobbies. If my present day self could speak to my younger self, or other single women, I would tell them, "When the time is right, the right person will show up. In the meantime, keep growing and keep moving forward. If you are a single parent, raise your children to the best of your abilities while not allowing them to shape their opinions and ideals from the artificial." My mother was a role model for me and did an excellent job with taking care of me. There were things I simply wanted that we did not have nor did my mother want for herself.

As for the relationship, I continued to ignore the warnings signs. Where do we end up when we ignore the signs? We often end up married with more children and the problems have gotten worse. Now, I am a married with twins and a toddler. My husband has managed to secure a job that removed him more than 50% of the time from the home. This is not the life I predicted when I watched the Jetsons. As an only child, I didn't have the experience of dealing with anybody other than myself. Becoming a mother not only to one child but three was a challenge and at times overwhelming. There were days where I couldn't even make a meal. I had no one to call or tell the truth. There was a foundation in which I belonged for mothers of multiples where I was able to share my feelings with one of the administrators. She personally made a meal of Chicken Divan and Rice for my family as a kind gesture. I will never forget that. I felt so helpless and hopeless that I couldn't be the strong mother and wife I'd hoped to be. I didn't realize that what that I had was postpartum depression. I was like a functioning alcoholic.

On a daily basis, I was struggling to keep from harming myself and my children. The thoughts were embarrassing, scary, and I didn't understand why I felt the way that I did. I can recall vividly, episodes of crying, and just wanting to lie in bed all day. Some days, I thought that if I would just stay in bed those babies would figure things out on their own. I knew I had to be their mother and make their bottles and change the diapers, but sometimes I felt like I was in quicksand. I was paralyzed with depression. I feel horrible to say it, but I almost hated my kids. I've done things that no one will ever know besides me and God. I was sick and I needed help.

One day, things were so out of control. My husband had to leave for work. I was angry at him because I needed help with the kids. I begged him to stay home for the day. When he refused and got in the car, I was just finishing changing one of the kids diapers. I was so angry that he was leaving, that I ran out of the door behind him and threw the dirty diaper on his windshield. That was a messy scene…. But nothing stopped him from leaving that day. That became a set up for what our future was going to look like.

As time progressed, I seemed to make it through some tough days but my marriage seemed to be another obstacle for me. I remember coming home one day eager to tell my husband what a good day I had and how much I was looking forward to contributing once again to our household. I had been a stay-at-home mom for a period of time. He walked into the kitchen where I was standing, in a calm, cool and collected voice and uttered the words, "I'm leaving." I was so clueless as to what he meant, that I said back to him, "Wherever you're going, bring me back something." I honestly thought he was going to the store or to a restaurant. He said again, "No Chanee, I'm leaving, it's over." It was like my life started moving in slow motion. I was shocked, dazed, and confused. How could this be? Leaving? To go where, why, how, and furthermore, with who? I couldn't comprehend what was happening, let alone how to react. All I could do was cry. I cried so hard and all he could say to me was, "This is how I knew you would react and this is why I didn't want to tell you." He didn't so much as hold me, he didn't wipe a single tear. For a while, I walked around in shock until I realized there was nothing I could do about it.

A couple of years past and my children and I had to make many adjustments to our new life but I'm so glad that God heard my prayers. He knew that I still wanted to be married to someone that would love me and accept my children. A man who didn't want more children, might I add. God blessed me with a man that loves God, loves me and my children. We were wed in holy matrimony on the island of Maui with the sun shining on us. As scripture states, " To everything there is a season, and a time to every purpose under the heaven," Ecclesiastes 3:1.

The pain continues to haunt me. Even though the first marriage is over, the pain is still real. The feelings stemming from abandonment are hurtful. At some point we have to fix the real problems which may be ourselves. We have to break those cycles and free ourselves so that we are not co-dependent. I can attest to not wanting to do things alone. I can look in the mirror at myself and see my flawed self. I was broken by past hurt, shame, regret, and simply not being perfect. I am learning how to turn the pain into power. There is more to accomplish and I love who I am becoming.

Take the first step to turning your pain into power by surrounding yourself with people that believe in you. Those who truly want the best for you and that have your better interest at heart, not those who rejoice in your misfortune. You'd be surprised that there are some people wagering on your loss rather than your gains. God has an assignment for all of us. It's been told to me that, "If you do not fulfill your assignment that's been given to you; God will see to it that you live long enough to see your replacement." Stay armed with the Word of God and prevail. If not, you will easily succumb to the temptations of the world. To move forward with the assignment God has for us can be uncomfortable. He will remove what is comfortable and familiar in order to force the assignment upon us. I am not sure how many of us can relate to losing a job and how uncomfortable it is to find a replacement.

One of the most important things I tell myself each day at this point in my life is to surround myself with those who get it. When we rid ourselves of the idea that we can change someone else's perception of us we free ourselves. We are then free to function and grow to our highest potenial. Some will never grasp the concept of true freedom or live freely. Nor will some live to fulfill their obligation to the world. Most people are too concerned with the thoughts of others and fearful of individual thought or being ostracized. It's much easier to follow the crowd than to stand alone and become a trailblazer or even worse- become ostracized themselves. Hopefully I am speaking to someone right now who can relate to pain caused by those you love. Yet, you can rise and find love and support from those that God has strategically placed in your life. I love to say, God did not bless me with brothers and sisters, but God has blessed me with amazing friends. It is because of many of them I have been able to overcome some of my darkest moments. I choose to turn that pain into power and move forward in life. It should be of utmost importance that we find out our true assignment in the world. Once we know the assignment, we must pursue our own truth and happiness.

Many of us, including myself, live with the notion that we must satisfy other people, live up to a standard or seek the approval of others. Some people simply won't like you based on who you are, but rather it is a reflection of who they are not. I've come to know more of my ability and those qualities that are admirable and use those in my quest for greatness. "Never waste time trying to explain yourself to those who are committed to misunderstanding you (Author unknown)." I really like that quote because, it applies to anyone; family, friends as well as strangers.

God has our hand and our steps are ordered. Psalm 37:23 KJV, "The steps of a good man are ordered by the LORD: and he delighteth in his way. " Put your faith and trust in the Lord and cast your cares upon him. He is the only one that can truly walk with you and help you turn your pain into power.

Rose Dunn

Rose Dunn is a saved, single mother of three beautiful children; her daughter Zuri age 23, and two sons Zarin and Stephen ages 19 and 15. It is said that Rose is calm, generous and always willing to help those who are in need. She has struggled and cried many tears over the years but with God's help she has made it through. Daily, Rose is becoming wiser with the guidance of the Holy Spirit.

She wrote this story to encourage you that it doesn't matter if your life started off rough, God will and does have the final say. He is the author of our story called life. He will complete the work He has started in us (Philippians 1: 6). For Booking Information, you can contact Rosa at dunnclassylady1@aol.com You can also find her on Twitter @RoseDun06414071.

THE ROSE THAT GREW FROM CONCRETE

by Rose Dunn

I was only sixteen when I met my ex-husband John at the club. I was a senior in high school and John was a junior. His mother kicked him out the house so my mother agreed to let him move in with us. Even though my mother talked to me time and time again about how special my virginity was and how once it was gone you could never get it back, I rationalized in my head that I was a senior in high school and that I was grown so I could make my own decisions. After he moved in I had sex with him. He was my first and I got pregnant. When my mother found out that we had sex she kicked John out the house. When I told her that I was pregnant she got so angry she started punching and kicking me in my stomach. She was so disappointed in me. I went to the abortion clinic three times and just couldn't make myself follow through.

During this time my mother went to prison. One morning as my mother was coming home she asked a man who lived in our building for a cigarette. Moments later we got a knock at the door and it's the lady who lived downstairs asking for my mom. Her husband was the one who gave mom the cigarette. When my mom came to the door the lady pulled a gun on mom and threatened her. She told my mom to stay away from her husband or she would kill her. The next day my mom went to her door to finish discussing the issue with a knife and stabbed the lady. The District Attorney pressed charges and my mother served 3 years in prison. The rest of our family was court ordered to move out of Long Beach so we moved to Norwalk were I started attending La Mirada Continuation School for Pregnant Teens.

In June I graduated from high school. I was eighteen and 9 months pregnant. I had my daughter in July. My mother, being locked up, missed my graduation and the birth of my daughter, but I had my grandmother, my baby sister and my aunt at my graduation for support. Once I had my daughter John came by to see her maybe once or twice and then he just disappeared. He was nowhere to be found for about two years after that. He decided he didn't want anything to do with our baby and ended up having a child with another girl.

After high school graduation and the birth of my daughter I decided to get job and enroll into Community College. With my mother still away in prison my grandmother helped me with my baby while I worked and went to school. When mom was released, she came home and began to look for John. She found him and convinced him that he needed to be with me and help raise his child so we ended up getting married.

John and I were married for about seven months when my mother went back to jail on a parole violation. During that time it was really hard on me because my mother was gone and I had my daughter and my little sister who was a freshman in high school to look after. My grandmother had moved out of town to take care of her boss's mother, so I was left to figure out how to be married, be a mother and big sister all on my own. John spent most of his time going to the studio, writing music and getting high on marijuana. At times I would be so frustrated with him and his lack of help with anything pertaining to the forward progression of our family that I wanted to hurt him. My mother in law tried to get us to move to Maryland with their family hoping that the change of scenery would help him do better, but I was afraid to go. My mother was still in prison and I didn't know any of his family. I didn't want to get trapped in a place where I had no family or people I knew. Once my mother was released John and I ended up splitting up only to find out that I was pregnant with my second child. That didn't stop him from moving out.

Once he moved I started dating my neighbor's cousin, Kevin. Kevin raised my newborn as his own. The relationship was good when we first started dating. We were both working and making pretty decent money. We were happy. But then, like all couples, things came up and we started to argue. Once, he made me so angry that I flattened all four of the tires on our car. We were young and I thought it was normal to do foolish things like that because that's what I grew up seeing in my home. I also tried to kick the front windshield out of our car one morning while Kevin was taking me to work.

Some mornings I would get to work so angry and wound up from arguing with him I would be angry at the world. I had a co-worker at the hospital. She would see me walking into work all mad and in the break room crying and she would come in and sit with me and ask me, "Why do you let that foolish man hurt you like that and allow him to make you act all crazy?" She would say to me, "You're a sweet girl and have to make a good life for you and your kids, Rose." She witnessed to me and asked if I knew Jesus, if I had accepted him into my life as my Lord and Savior? I told her that I used to go to the Kingdom Hall but I wasn't sure that if I died at that moment that I was going to heaven. She had me ask Jesus into my life and confess my sins right there in the break room at work. Kevin and I had been in a five year relationship when I gave my life to Christ. Kevin was the father of my youngest child and he promised that we would get married after I had the baby. We never got married.

After I accepted Jesus into my life I just needed some peace, and I felt something tugging me to go to church. I remembered my aunt's church in Los Angeles where my family would go sometimes when she would invite us for Family and Friends Day. I called her up and asked her if I could come to church? I started attending church regularly. I could only attend Sunday school because we only had one car and Kevin would fuss and say,

"Don't leave me in the house all day with no car." Whenever I would go to Sunday school it seemed like the lesson was speaking just to me and my situation. I didn't know anyone at the church besides my aunt and uncle so I knew that no one knew what was going on at home. When I went I would leave church with so much peace, then go home and be right back in the middle of the mess and stress. The more I went to church the more I felt the Holy Spirit leading me to get out of the relationship. I was so afraid to leave because I didn't think that I could make it on my own without the financial support of Kevin. I called my mother and told her I wanted to move. She wasn't a big fan of Kevin and our relationship anyway, so she came with my cousin and they moved me out the house within a few hours. By the end of the week I let Kevin talk me into moving right back home.

As soon as I moved back in I got pregnant with my youngest child and Kevin and I began to argue and fight every day. It got so bad that my oldest daughter began to act out at school. It seemed like the school was calling me every day. I knew at that point that I had made a huge mistake moving back but I didn't know what to do.

After nine months of arguing and fighting and having the most stressful pregnancy I could have imagined, Kevin and I got into a bad fight and I moved out to my brother's house leaving everything behind except the kids and our clothes. At this point I was looking for my own place and had to go back to work, cutting my maternity leave short. While I was on leave the company I worked for was bought out by another company and I was laid off. I had to look for a new job. God blessed me to find a job doing medical billing and a one bedroom apartment that I could afford on my own in the city of Bellflower.

As I began to grow closer and closer to the Lord it seemed as though I was always getting tested. The building I lived in was so rowdy and ghetto the people would just pick fights with me and my kids. One kid picked on my oldest son and tried to fight him just so I could come out side and get into a fight with his mom. It was crazy. God really allowed me to go through six tough years living in that apartment building, teaching me how to hold my tongue and be a peacemaker, and learn how to resolve conflict without fighting. This was especially hard for me because I was a fighter.

Eventually God blessed me with a new job making more money and an apartment in a much nicer area. I was a witness to the scripture that says God will make your enemies your foot stool (Luke 20:43) when my rowdy neighbors saw me blessed with a new car, a new job and nice things before I moved. God even allowed my son to win a fight with that bully days before we moved and to this day when they see each other in the neighborhood he shows nothing but respect to my son.

Life was good and things were coming together. I was living good and saved for about five years until I hit a bend in the road. I met this man who I fell madly in love with. I was so obsessed with him all I did was fantasize about him all day. I was so focused on this man that I began to ignore Gods voice speaking to me. I allowed my mind be consumed with thoughts of him all day.

During this time I was laid off my job again and did not find a permanent position this time. I was only able to obtain a temporary position doing medical billing. I was under so much stress that I became ill and was off of work for about a week. I was working temp. I didn't get benefits like medical and vacation time. When I got paid my check was so small I didn't have enough to pay all my bills so I paid my rent with the money I had but my truck got repossessed. The next month I took part of my rent money and got my truck out of impound. As a result I didn't have all my rent money, so I had to move.

From there my children and I moved with my cousin in Los Angeles and stayed with her for a few months. During that time my daughter, who was about thirteen, didn't take us losing our place too well. Zuri started rebelling by running away to friend's house. I would send the police for her so her friend's parents would send her home.

After a few months my cousin ended up telling me to move out over a money disagreement. From there we moved in with my sister and stepfather. Someone in my family reported me an unfit mother to children's services and tried to have my children taken away from me. Children's services came to my stepfather's house and questioned my children and I asking if I spanked my kids. I told them I did whip my kids if they were misbehaving. My kids told the social worker the same thing, "My momma whip us when we're bad." DPCS closed the case and I never heard anything else from the social worker. I was so hurt and angry at my mother and my sister and a few other family members because I knew that one of them had called children's services on me. My mother was telling me that I was a bad mom because I was obsessing over a man and that's why I lost my place and my job. She said that God was punishing me for being disobedient for putting man before God and that I was going crazy.

I hit rock bottom and didn't know why I was going through all these things but I knew that God was not going to leave me like this. I decided to go back to school. I started out full time at first but then eventually reduced the load, going part time while working part time. After moving out of my stepfather's place my brother had a condo for sale so he let me and the kids stay there while waiting for a buyer. While staying at my brother's condo a shelter in San Pedro called me and told me they had space for me and the kids. I had been on the waiting list for about two months. I was expecting to wait for the shelter to call me in ninety days but they ended up calling me in sixty days. This was only God.

Right before they called me my mother and I got into the worse argument we ever had. We were both yelling back and forth at each other and my kids were crying and I even ended up swearing at her. Now this was really bad because I had not used profanity since God saved me and filled me with His Spirit five years ago. My kids didn't understand it; they never heard me talk like that before. It really had the kids upset. My mother and I were arguing about a towel that I used. Yes, a stupid towel: It was insane. My mother called my brother and told him that I was fighting with her so he would put me out of his condo, which he did. But right after he told me I had to leave the shelter called me telling me they had room for me and the kids.

The shelter that we stayed in was a ninety day homeless shelter for families. If we followed the rules which were to attend weekly meetings, be inside by 9 pm, no visitors, no drinking, drugs and save 80% of our income they would submit our paper work to the housing program for homeless families.

It was here at the shelter that the Lord led me to feed the homeless. I would make four plates that represented my kids and I out of whatever I cooked for that Saturday. Then we would ride down the street and offer the meals to the first four homeless people we would see. Some of the homeless people would take the meal and some of them didn't. I wanted to show my kids that although we were living in a shelter that there were people out there still in worse off situations than us. I wanted my children to be thankful that we had a nice shelter to stay in, not a nasty, dirty place where we would have to sleep on our stuff to prevent theft. Some shelters were pretty rough. God was with me while we were staying at the shelter by blessing me to win an appeal for unemployment.

Having to save 80% of our income didn't leave me very much income to work with. I had a six cylinder truck at the time and gas had gone up to four dollars a gallon and I was driving to Downey which was about 20 miles one way Monday through Friday. God made a way for me to have the money to buy gas.

After ninety days at the shelter we spent thirty days living with my ex, Kevin, until my housing paper work was processed. I was blessed with a newly built three bedroom home in Los Angeles. We were so happy to be back in our own home, but I was still angry at my family for the way they treated me when I was homeless. I was especially angry with my mother and my sister. A few months passed when I cut off all communications and didn't speak to my mother.

I remember getting tired of being angry all the time with my mother, so I began to pray and ask God to help me not be angry with her. I remember asking God to help me to be able to have a relationship with my mom, because at that point I realized that she was not going to change the way she was. I asked God to change me so I could have a relationship with her. A close friend of mine had lost her mother suddenly to a brain aneurism. I didn't want my mother to die with us being angry and not speaking to each other. Today, she and I are in a much better place with an understanding.

Once we were settled in our new place my daughter, Zuri, begin to calm down and focus on school and stop getting into trouble. She apologized to me and said she was going to do better, which she did. We lived in Los Angeles for about a year but then I noticed that the guys in the neighborhood started asking my sons where they lived. I didn't want the neighborhood guys to try to recruit my boys into a gang so we moved back to the city of Paramount.

While living in Paramount I met a younger man that I dated and let move in with me and the kids. I thought I was doing something because my daughter had just graduated from high school and I felt like I could move a man in and do what I wanted to do and live how I wanted to live. God allowed me to act out for so long but he would not let me go. I ended up getting pregnant. I was so devastated and embarrassed that I got pregnant that I aborted the baby because I didn't want anyone to know how I was living behind closed doors. Being a Christian I was devastated that I even got myself in that situation. I was burdened with guilt and shame. That's when I hit an all-time low.

I reached out to a friend and asked her to take me to church. She brought me to the place where I currently worship and call home. This was such a blessing because I was so broken when I joined. As time has passed I healed in the areas I was once broken.

I have learned valuable lessons from the pain and process that God has allowed me to go through. The most important advice I can pass along from my experience is that God really does love us and he cares and he only desires what is best for us. God will use the decisions we make, good and or bad, to prosper our souls. Even if we go through difficulties, which we all will at some time in our lives, at the end of it all we can look back and see God's hand and how He has kept us and is protecting and covering us all along the way. Be encouraged; stay encouraged. The season that you may be in right now too shall pass. Stay with God and go through your storm, test or trial because your victory is on the other side.

Denice M. Burkhardt

Denice is a conference speaker that inspires and empowers others to reach above and beyond their wildest dreams. She encourages singles not to settle for mediocrity and to wait on God's Best. Denice keeps it 100% as she speaks the compelling and uncompromising truth about abstinence, choices, and consequences. Furthermore, she transparently ministers to others by sharing her powerful testimony on a one to one basis, in small groups or conference settings on Grieving the Loss of a Loved One.

Denice is the CEO of Str8 from D'Hardt Gourmet Salads. These Delicious Healthy Salads have aided in her amazing weight loss journey of seventy-five pounds and counting. In addition to working full-time for a company leading the health care industry, she also serves faithfully at Most Holy Place Community Church in the beautiful city of Lake Elsinore, California as Executive Assistant to Lady Rhonda Culton. Denice is a go-getter and is always striving to go from Good to Great. Her academic accomplishments include: A Master of Science in Marital and Family Therapy, Bachelor of Arts in Psychology, Bachelor of Science in Business Administration and lastly, she is an Organizational Leadership Doctoral Candidate.

For speaking engagements or Str8 from D'Hardt Gourmet Salads you may contact Denice Burkhardt at www.deniceburkhardt.com, denice@deniceburkhardt.com, Facebook, Twitter, Instagram and Pinterest.

BROKEN BUT NOT BEYOND REPAIR:

GRIEVING THE LOSS OF A LOVED ONE

by Denice M. Burkhardt

At thirteen years of age, I was frantically awakened as I heard screaming coming from downstairs. "No! No!" As I jumped up and ran down stairs in a panic, I was not prepared for what greeted me as I turned the corner. My Dad, face down on the floor and it appeared that his underclothes were soiled. My Mom was hysterical beyond control as the paramedics rushed in to attempt to resuscitate my Dad. I was quickly whisked away from the scene and taken across the street to my neighbor's house. I remember sitting on my neighbor's couch for hours wondering helplessly, "What in the world happened to my Dad?" I remember like it was yesterday, it seemed like I was at my neighbor's house for an eternity. I finally summed up enough courage to get off the couch and look out the garage door. When I saw the coroner's truck in the driveway, I knew my life as it was, would never be the same. Without any warning, my Dad suddenly died of a heart attack at the early age of forty-seven. What A tragedy! This is not how I intended to spend my Veteran's Day holiday. I went to sleep as Daddy's Little Princess and just like that, I woke up fatherless. How do I move forward?

Over the course of the next week, neighbors, friends from church and my Dad's co-workers stopped by to express their condolences and brought over food and sympathy cards. Some of the ministers and members from the church assisted my Mom with funeral arrangements. To date, we still cannot figure out who had the unmitigated gall to steal close to four thousand dollars from the trunk of my Mother's car as she prepared to pay for funeral expenses. We were already emotionally distraught, but this took my Mom to another dimension. I am not sure how my brother took the sudden loss of my Dad, but he was unable to attend the funeral. On the eve of laying my father to rest, the spirit in the house felt like a gloomy severe sense of emptiness and hopelessness.

I went back to the room where my father was found dead and relived that horrific moment. In my finite mind, I could not figure out why I saw feces in my Dad's underwear. (According to the medical dictionary when a person dies the internal and external anal sphincter muscle controlling the opening and closing of the anus becomes incapacitated and they defecate.) For a moment I just looked up toward heaven with a blank stare wondering, "Who's going to walk me down the aisle when I get married and who in the world am I going to do the Father-Daughter dance with at my wedding?" I finally went to sleep as I soaked my pillow case with tears of sorrow.

In the morning I protested in my inner dialogue how

I wished I could awake from this tumultuous nightmare, but ready or not, it was time to lay my Dad to rest. On the day of the funeral, the police presence was out in full force to support one of their fellow comrades. Police cars, men in uniform, sirens and red lights flashing for as far as I could see. During the funeral procession I fantasized about what I would give to see my Dad sitting behind the wheel of one of those police cars again or to bring me some Winchell's Donuts home or to take my brother and I to McDonald's. Lord just one more day! I did not even get a chance to say goodbye, to hug his neck or to tell my Dad I loved him before he died. No! This is not Fair! Why is this happening to me!

Without having any say-so, my grieving mother instantaneously became a single mother of two teenagers. There have been several people that have impacted my life, but nothing like my strong and courageous Mom. My Mom lost twenty pounds over a three week period. She was so incredibly devastated that she lost her appetite. Nevertheless, she kept the family intact.

My father could no longer pick us up from school, so she immediately arranged for us to walk over a close family friend's house to await her arrival. We were very fortunate to attend one of the top achieving schools in another district. Although we went from a two household income down to one, we never lacked any food, shelter or clothing. My Mother was my guardian angel. I was totally unprepared for the sudden passing of my father, but she held my hand tightly until I could stand on my own two feet again. My mother spent several hours instilling in me the importance of acting like a lady and valuing myself. She talked about sex, keeping my dress down, my panties up and a plethora of other topics. I felt very special when my mother presented me with a commitment ring and a contract to remain pure until marriage. I went on to successfully complete middle school with honors and advanced to high school.

Looking back, although I excelled academically, I failed miserably at my eating habits after the loss of my Dad. My Mom and I were on opposite ends of the spectrum, she lost a significant amount a weight in a short period of time and I gained several pounds. At the time I did not realize I was trying to fill a void with food. I was not only grieving the loss of my Dad, but I had just involuntarily become a statistic of fatherlessness. I lost my covering, my provider, my protector and king of the household. I remember feverishly overindulging in comfort foods like fried chicken, Hawaiian Sweet Rolls, potato chips, hamburgers, and french fries. I felt like I could never quite satisfy my hunger. (This is an area to be very aware of while you are grieving the loss of a loved one, it can easily become an eating disorder.) I was not in any form or fashion cognizant of how much food I was consuming. My mother enjoyed cooking and always cooked like she was feeding an army. There were no limits set on how much food I could have, but beyond a shadow of a doubt, whatever I put on my plate I had better eat it all or I was in big trouble.

My mother was always a beacon of light at her job, at church, and in the community. The next chapter of my journey, The Challenge, manifested in the form of my mother's bout with cancer. Not only did her life drastically change after being diagnosed with cancer, but mine did as well. It was thrust upon me to become head of household and caregiver in an instant. I worried about how I was going to go to work, take my mother to all her chemotherapy appointments, complete my dissertation, pay my bills and cook. After several rounds of chemotherapy and surgery my mother fully recovered. Thereafter, life as I had known it returned to normal. Two years later the cancer returned, but this time it proved to be inoperable. After coming to the realization that she was never coming home from the hospital, I went to the funeral home to make final arrangements. My mother fought with every ounce of strength she had to stay on earth. Even after the plug was pulled from life support, she fought to stay alive another twelve hours. It was as if she argued with God that it was not time for her to go. It was an honor to care for my mother and to take her to every doctor and chemotherapy appointment.

To date, my mother's death has been my greatest

challenge, The Abyss. I was confronted with how to move forward after losing my best friend the one with whom I could share my most intimate deep secrets. I unwillingly had to surrender myself completely to the process of this adventure and become one with it. I'm grateful I had the strength to seek professional counseling three weeks after my mother's death, or I would have completely fallen apart. Upon return from the journey, I brought back several gifts with me. My mother taught me that I can be an agent of change on my job, without losing respect and dignity. I also learned that when unexpected life events occur, one can get through them with the help of God, professional therapists and spiritual guidance. Some days I did not want to get out of bed or go to work. I was not clinically depressed, but heavily grieving. Just coming into my teen years was a very crucial time to lose my father. My mother spared me years of agony when she presented me with a commitment ring and a contract to remain pure until marriage.

Other gifts I brought back with me were high self-esteem and self-respect. Although my father suddenly passed away, my mother stressed that it was of the utmost importance to keep my grades up and graduate with honors. In essence, she was saying, even if your father was still here on earth, he would not be going to class for you or studying for your exams. Even before I was born my mother set a high standard and lead by example, as shown when she graduated Valedictorian of her high school. One of the most important lessons I learned from my mother's passing was the art of surrendering. As she lay helpless in her hospital bed, in severe pain, I constantly prayed and cried out to God to heal every cancerous cell in her body. As her caregiver, I did everything I possibly could do to keep her here on earth, but I had to finally surrender complete control to God. I will always count it an honor and a privilege to have had the strength and courage to usher my Mother to the gates of heaven.

At the age of thirteen my Dad dies without any warning and now my Mom is dead. Really ? I was so angry at God. I felt like I had been betrayed by the man who I totally and completely put my trust in. I asked over and over again, God, how could you allow this to happen? I shared this excerpt on Facebook and so many were blessed by my transparency that I thought it would be befitting to include in my chapter.

What Happens When God Says "No" to your Prayers? On this day a few years ago I was an emotional wreck as I was preparing to lay to rest my beautiful Mom, Evangelist Inez V. Burkhardt. I was so angry at God...God!!! How could you let this happen? Why did you let this happen? I just could not comprehend how my Mom could be used as a vessel to lay hands on the sick and they recovered, but she died. Lord!!! What is going on? You said in your word, By His stripes we are healed and no weapon formed against us shall prosper. Lord Why? She obeyed your word, she was an excellent mother and wife and she diligently sought your face every morning when she arose. God!!! She was a yielded vessel that allowed the gift of the Holy Spirit to flow through her. Whether it be at church, the grocery or just talking to a neighbor or stranger she spoke prophetically and people were sometimes slain in the spirit. Lord!!! How could you let this great woman of God die? This is not fair!!!! Without warning my Dad died when I was 13. Now this!!!! I know we are not supposed to question where God puts a period, but I did. Lord!!! I need her!!! How do you go from cruising and traveling around the world, shopping escapades, mother and daughter weekends, getting facials and massages to multiple doctor appointments, chemotherapy to treat uterine cancer, severe weakness, excessive weight loss and decreased appetite? There are evil people out there shooting, stabbing and killing right and left without consequence. God!!!! Why her? Lord!!! Where are you? You said you would never leave us nor forsake us. Why have you abandoned me? If another person comes up to me and say's "she's in a better place or to absent from the body is to be present with the Lord I am going to scream"! I know they meant well, but those words were not comforting me. This is exactly how I felt when my Mom died.

Ohhhhhh, but today, today, today I am happy to report, I am not where I want to be, but I can say with assurance, I am not where I used to be. My joy and peace that surpasses all understanding has been restored. I have been monitoring my emotions every day since last Friday, the date my Mom passed and I am doing well mentally, physically and emotionally. I took the necessary steps I needed to take to address the hole in my soul. I know Therapy may be frowned upon by some churches and some cultures, but I had to do what I needed to do for me. Some turn to alcohol, drugs, food or sex to numb the pain, but that's only a temporary solution that is detrimental to your health.

Three weeks after the death of my Mom, I sought Grief Therapy in a group setting and it proved to be very beneficial for me. I have to admit, I was somewhat embarrassed to be a degreed Marital and Family Therapist reaching out for help, but here's the thing; I was not in denial about the fact that I needed help. This was something that I could not just pray away or go to the altar and turn around 3 times and it was over. No!!!! Losing a mother is a traumatic experience and I had to go through the grieving process. In addition to grief therapy, I started journaling my feelings, which I found to be very cathartic and in honor of my mother, I volunteered at the hospital where she died. Everyone's journey will be a little different than the next, but I firmly believe, earth has no sorrow Heaven cannot heal. I promise you, couple prayer with the process and it will get better with time. I am praying that this may help someone grieving the loss of a loved one.

Lamentations 3:22-23 (NKJV) states "Through the Lord's mercies we are not consumed, because His compassion's fail not. They are new every morning; Great is Your faithfulness." I thank God for new mercies every morning. After the loss of a loved one there is hope to regain your balance once again. Life will deal you a series of unexpected blows, but who you lean on in times of uncertainty makes a huge difference. First, acknowledge that you are broken. (Merriam-Webster's Dictionary defines broken as separated in to parts or pieces by being hit.) The death of a loved one shatters hopes and dreams, but I can personally say, you can pick up the pieces and begin again. God can take every cracked, fragile piece of your heart and mend it back together again. I will admit that I am still being processed. Please be aware the healing process takes time. When it comes to grieving the loss of a loved one I want to reiterate, there is no such thing as go to the altar and turn around three times and it's over. "Weeping may endure for a night, but joy comes in the morning," Psalm 30:5. Morning comes at different times depending on who you are. If you surrender to God with every fiber of your being, these afflictions of sorrow can and will be eclipsed by God's Glory.

God has really been Faithful to me. As a result of my volunteering at the hospital where my Mother died, I was blessed to be hired full-time. Earlier I spoke about gaining a substantial amount of weight after the death of my Dad. I never did quite get back down to my normal weight, but after the death of my Mother I really packed on the pounds. I unconsciously ballooned up to 300 lbs., however, I am happy to report to date I have lost seventy-five plus pounds and counting. To God Be the Glory! Today, I am a committed pescetarian, I no longer consume red meat, pork, chicken or turkey and I get in my exercise three to five times a week. My life is back on track and I literally feel 21 all over again.

I would like to dedicate this chapter to my precious parents Robert L. Burkhardt and Inez V. Burkhardt and my spiritual parents Pastor Fabian M. Culton and Lady Rhonda Culton. As I share my authentic testimony I pray this encourages someone to get healed as they are going through the grieving process. Truth be told, grief is never something you get over, you just learn how to get through it on a day-to-day basis.

PRAYER

Father God, I don't understand why my loved one had to leave so soon, but Lord I trust you. Lord, you said in your Word that I am to trust you with all my heart and lean not to my own understanding. Lord show me how to move forward and cast all my cares on you when I am emotionally spent. When a spirit of depression tries to come upon me, Father God, give me the strength to cast it down in the name of Jesus. Lord, bless me with friends I can share my most intimate thoughts, without being judged. Father God, above all else, keep my mind and continue to restore my joy and peace. Fill the void around holidays and birthdays when no one is there. Lord allow me to be cognizant of what and how much food I am consuming. Lastly, give me the courage to be an example to others, that with much prayer and supplication in the Master's Hand, God can put the broken pieces back together again. — Amen.

Charlie Randle-Pride
Queen Charlie

Queen Charlie is a native of Cleveland, Ohio. She has been married to Dr. Albert Pride, Jr. for 23 years. Together they have 5 children, 16 grandchildren, and 2 great grandsons. She and her husband served at Christian Faith Ministry in ministry in Long Beach, California for 15 years before returning to their hometown of Cleveland, Ohio.

Queen Charlie loves the Lord, her husband, her children, and especially her grandchildren. In her spare time, she finds comfort in the Bible, makeup artistry, romantic music, cold weather, computers, and traveling. Her desire is to travel to Africa in the near future to discover her royal roots. *Inspire* is her first writing project. She hopes to write her own book one day. You can contact her at queencharlie528@gmail.com.

I HEARD MAMA SAY

by Charlie Randle-Pride

It was bitter cold that day. It was dark outside. I was at the bus stop standing there doing my best to keep warm and look out for the bus. The people at the bus stop were huddling together on the bench. There is something so foreboding about being in the dark in the cold, at the bus stop on Kinsman Avenue, in the urban jungle of Cleveland, Ohio, but my appointment at the welfare office was early in the morning. If I wanted to keep my money and food stamps coming, I had to get there on time. The bus was slow coming. For what seemed like the hundredth time, I looked up the street. The bus was finally coming.

As I was stepping up on the bus, I thought about my mother. I thought about how she would get up at the crack of dawn when the birds were still sleeping, and the night was still enveloping the streets to go to work. She never complained about the weather, or her job, or the fact that she was struggling to raise the eight of us in the worst projects in Cleveland. She always kept it going whether sick or discouraged. She just knew that she was the breadwinner, and that she had do what she had to do to keep our heads above water. I used to wonder how she did so much with so little. What was it that kept her going? Until one day, as she was going out the door to stand in the cold darkness at the bus stop, I heard Mama say, "And with the grace of God go I."

The bus driver opened the door. It looked like folks were about to fall out the door. I had to get on that bus. I could not be late. I knew that if I arrived there late, my appointment would be rescheduled. Then, my check and food stamps would be delayed. Lord knows that I did not need that. The bus driver yelled, "Please go to the back!" There was standing room only. I was standing and holding on to the overhead rails in the back of the bus. As I looked down, I noticed a young lady sitting in the seat right under me. She looked like she was my age. It looked like she was on her way to work or somewhere important. Her makeup was perfect. She had on a nice pair of boots and a very nice winter coat. She had a Coach bag, and a real leather briefcase. She was reading a book by Maya Angelou. She looked happy, peaceful, and successful. I wondered who she worked for and what kind of work she did. One thing was for sure, I knew that she wasn't on her way to the welfare office to see a case worker like I was.

I don't know why, but observing this young lady made me begin reflecting on my own life. I managed to graduate from high school. I attended college for a short time. But, there I was with two kids, and two baby daddies. We were living in the worse housing projects in Cleveland.

My only saving grace was that my family lived down the street from me. They helped keep my head above water. I was thankful for that.

"Next stop, Public Square!" the bus driver yelled. I made my way to the back door to exit. People were pushing and shoving. After all, we all had a destination to get to, and things to do. The young woman, who had got me to thinking about my life, was in front of me. I watched her as she left the bus and walked down the street and out of my sight. For some strange reason, I thought about her a lot that day.

After walking for what seemed a year in the cold and snow, I finally made it to the welfare office. What a frustrating experience! I hated going down there! Unfortunately, I didn't have much choice. People and children were everywhere. I could barely find a seat. It seemed like all of the seats were taken. There was no way that I was going to stand up and wait my turn to see the case worker. So, I went back into the hallway and there was an empty chair. I ran to get that seat! As I sat there, I began to think what if my name was called and I didn't hear it? The way it worked was if they called your name, and you didn't answer, you were counted as a no-show and they would shut your case down. Lord knew that I could not have that happen! That was the last thing that I needed. My food was low, and the kids needed new shoes and clothes, I was behind with my rent, and I couldn't find a decent job. I felt like my life was a mess. I heard my Mama say, "And with the grace of God go I."

As I sat there waiting to see a case worker, I thought about the girl on the bus. She made me think about how I felt like I was going nowhere fast. I chastised myself because I should have been just like her. It should have been me sitting on the bus looking like a business woman on her way to work. I asked myself, "Where did you go wrong? You're a high school graduate. You were smart in school. You have some college under your belt. Your grades were decent when you wanted them to be. But you quit! You allowed life to toss you to and fro!" I heard my Mama say, "And with the grace of God go I."

It was lunch time. All of a sudden, the case workers started coming from the back and going out of the door. My case worker was one of them. I said to myself, "What the hell! She's going to lunch! That means that I will have to sit here for almost the whole day to see her! That's crazy! I had an appointment!" I heard my Mama say, "And with the grace of God go I."

I accepted the fact that I would be there for a while and might as well get something out of the vending machine. I found two dollars and some change in my purse. I was praying that there would be something I could afford in the vending machine. So, I took a chance. I found a sandwich for two bucks! I put my two dollars in the machine. The sandwich turned on the carousel to the out door as it should, but when I tried to open the door, it wouldn't budge. I yelled, "What is wrong with this machine! That was my last two dollars!"

The security guard came over to see what was going on. He tried to get the sandwich out of the machine. The door would not budge. He told me that I would have to submit a refund request for my money. I sighed, "Oh Lawd! I'm hungry! That was my last two dollars!" I wanted to cry! I guess the security guard felt sorry for me. He offered to buy my lunch, but I refused his offer. Then he said, "Let me bless you!" When he said that, my heart opened up immediately. I accepted his lunch offer, and I thanked him for his help. I heard my Mama say, "And with the grace of God go I."

Lunch time was over. I hurried back to the waiting area. It was still crowded. I looked for a seat. Finally! There was an empty seat way in the back of the room. I ran to get that seat. I sat down and pulled out the old newspaper that I had found in the vending area. The headline said, "Young Man Shot on the Eastside." Oh Lord! Another black man killed in his own neighborhood! I asked myself, "When will we stop killing each other?" My son was a little boy, but I was already worried that he would wind up dead like so many other young black men at that time. We lived in the projects on the east side of Cleveland, and chances were more likely than not that my son would get caught up in the madness and chaos of living on the east side, Black, and probably get killed! The very thought haunted me daily especially as he grew older. One of my biggest dreams was to get out of the projects and off of the east side of Cleveland before he got any older. But, how was I going to do that on welfare! How was I going to do that without a decent paying job? How was I going to do that with no husband? How was I going to do something when I was always thinking that I couldn't do anything? I heard my Mama say, "And by the grace of God go I."

The woman next to me noticed the headline on the newspaper about another killing. She just shook her head. "That's a damn shame!" she said. "My son got killed out there in these damn streets. He was just sixteen. Now he's dead and gone!" I could see the tears begin to swell in her eyes as she lamented her son's untimely death. I said, "Miss, I'm so sorry!" A tear rolled down her face. I gave her a tissue from my purse. As she wiped the tears from her haggard face, she said that she was there to make some adjustments to her welfare case since he had died. "Well," she said, "that's less money for me to make it out here. I was barely getting enough with him on my check, and now he's gone. I don't know what I'm going to do to replace that money. I just don't know what I'm going to do. My family had to hold car washes, bake sales, and take donations just to get enough money to bury him decent." Her story just reminded me of how determined I had to be to get my kids out of the projects and off the east side, or wind up like this woman mourning the death of her murdered son.

I thought to myself, "Her son is dead and she's worried about her welfare check money being reduced." All I could do was shake my head because it was reality for way too many black women. As she continued to tell her story, my name was called. "Saved by the welfare clerk!" I said to myself. I heard Mama say, "And with the grace of God go I."

The caseworker greeted me with a fake smile. I could tell that she had an attitude already. "Whatever!" I said under my breath. "You ain't getting on my nerve today lady!" I greeted her back with a fake smile too. I wasn't going to let her attitude push my buttons though. I said a brief prayer to the Lord to help me do and say the right things. As I reached her desk, she offered me a chair. I sat down and the inquisition began. I heard my Mama say, "And with the grace of God go I."

"Do you have all of the papers I asked you to bring for your redetermination today?" the case worker asked. I gave her the papers. "Now, Miss Randle, is all of your information the same? Are you still receiving financial aid for college?" I told her that I hadn't received any financial aid since I had dropped out of school at the beginning of the year. The next thing that came out of her mouth made me so mad that I wanted to punch her in the face! "Well, Miss Randle, financial aid is considered income. So, we're going to cut your food stamps from two hundred fifty dollars a month down to fifty dollars a month."

I looked at her so hard that if looks really could kill, she would have been dead under her seat! "Fifty dollars!" I said furiously. "What the hell am I supposed to do with fifty dollars a month to feed myself and two kids?"

"Well," she said. "Financial aid is considered income even if it does go straight to the school. Did you get a refund check?"

I leaned into her closer and looked straight into her blurry brown eyes and said, "Listen lady, that money goes toward clothes, shoes, and underwear for my kids. It lets me buy household stuff that I otherwise could not afford. Damn! Can't I get a break from y'all? I thought welfare was here to help folk. Instead, y'all cut people down every chance you get! How can anybody get ahead like that?"

She looked at me, "Well Miss Randle, that's just the way it is. If you don't like it, then you can always stop going to school."

"Then what? Am I supposed to live in the projects forever, and depend on some imaginary knight in shining armor to come along and rescue me and my kids? I don't think so!"

"Well, Miss Randle." I was getting tired of her saying, "Well, Miss Randle." "Your food stamps will be the only part of your benefits to be reduced. Your check will remain the same."

I let out a sigh of relief as I learned that my check would not be cut.

"Just sign these papers Miss Randle. These changes will be reflected in your benefits next month." What could I do? I felt trapped in the welfare system. There was no use in trying to fight the system. I signed the paper, and got the hell out of that stupid welfare office. I heard my Mama say, "And with the grace of God go I.

Well, I made it out of the welfare office before the traffic got bad. The bus wasn't as crowded as it was that morning. I found a seat by the window, and started thinking about how I was going to escape the cycle of welfare. My mother had to raise eight kids by herself on welfare. Now, here I was continuing the cycle. At least I had graduated from high school. But, nonetheless, I was caught up in the welfare trap. I didn't like it! I wanted out! I did not want to see my children in the same trap. It was that day that I made up my mind that I could do better. I had to do better! I heard my Mama say, "And with the grace of God go I."

I made it to my Mother's house. My kids were happy to see me. Mama asked me how it went at the welfare office. "Mom, you know how degrading it is to go down there! It was crowded. It seemed like it took forever to be seen. The case worker cut my food stamps! How am I going to feed us on fifty dollars a month?"

Mama asked me, "What happened to make them cut you off like that?"

I said, "Mom, you are not going to believe this crap. My case worker told me that receiving financial aid for school is considered income. Because of that, she cut my food stamps! What am I supposed to do?"

My mother looked at me and shook her head. She said, "Girl, where is your faith? I've seen you go through worse situations than this one! You're carrying on like it's the end of the world child!"

My Mother asking me about my faith woke me out of my ranting and raving about my food stamps. She reminded me that it was God's grace that always makes a way for me and my children. It was His grace that kept food on the table and clothing on our backs. It was His grace that kept a roof over our heads. It was His grace that protected me from the darkness of living in public housing. It was His grace that kept me from falling into the pit of despair. It was God's grace that was holding me up and giving me direction with my every step

"By the way," Mama said, "I was listening to the radio the other day, and there was an announcement from the Urban League that they are opening a new office training program next month. They're accepting applications next Monday. Ain't nothing good going to just fall into your lap! Go and get what God has for you!"

I said, "Thanks for looking out for me Mom. I will call them tomorrow. I know that the Lord will provide." I heard my Mama say, "And with the grace of God go I."

The next day, I called the Urban League. The woman on the other end explained to me that the announcement on the radio was for their new office training and word processing program. She asked me if I could type. I said, "Yes." I was glad that I had scrimped and saved to purchase a typewriter the month before to practice my typing. At the time, I didn't really know why I was buying a typewriter. Little did I know that God was preparing me for a new blessing. The woman on the phone from the Urban League gave me an appointment to come in the next day. She reminded to bring my high school diploma, social security card, and identification, and dress in business attire.

My interview day at the Urban League arrived. I could hardly sleep the night before. There wasn't much "business attire" in my closet for an interview, but I managed to find a black skirt, and white blouse, and a black sweater in my closet. I had a pair of black flats. There was my business attire for the interview. I grabbed my purse, and coat and headed out the door to catch the bus. I could hear my Mama say, "And with the grace of God go I."

The bus was running slow because of the falling snow. I managed to make it to the Urban League early. I practically fell through the door from running from the bus stop. Almost out of breath, I stopped at the desk to check in for my appointment. The receptionist escorted me to a room and told me that someone would be with me soon. I was nervous as all get out!

Five minutes later, a woman and a man entered where I was sitting. They introduced themselves to me as Roberta and Don. Roberta was from IBM, and Don was the director of the training program. I gave them my resume. They looked it over, and asked me different questions about my goals. I shared with them that my main reason for wanting to be a part of the program was so that I could get a better paying job and get off welfare. They both agreed that that was a great goal. But then, they asked me did I know that the age limit was 25. I was 26 at the time. I said that I didn't know that. I could feel my enthusiasm dwindling fast. Suddenly, I heard my Mama's voice say, "Where is your faith?" I began to pray. Roberta looked at me and said, "We really like you! You have a great personality, and you have some work experience. We believe that you have what it takes to go through the program. So, consider yourself accepted into the program. Congratulations!" She told me that classes started that next Monday, at 8am. I heard Mama say, "And with the grace of God go I."

I was so excited! I couldn't wait to tell my Mama. When I got to her house to get the kids I yelled out ,"I got in! I got in!"

Mama said , "See what happens when we go with the grace of God, and we walk by faith. Nothing is impossible with God!"

That was thirty years ago. I finished the program at the top of the class. I was hired by IBM straight out of the program. After IBM, I worked at several corporate locations in Cleveland, Ohio. They were all good paying jobs using the skills that I learned at the Urban League. I moved my family from the projects to a better neighborhood and better schools. I bought my first car too! The training that I received from the Urban League placed me on the path to a better life.

Now, I can say right along with my Mama, "And with the grace of God go I." For I know that His grace has kept me. With all of my heart I can say and mean that there's nothing impossible with God! If he did it for me, I know that He will do it for you! "ALL THINGS WORK TOGETHER FOR GOOD to those who love the Lord and are called according to His purpose," Romans 8:28. Amen!

Jill Elam

Jill Elam is a wife, daughter, sister, proud aunt, godmother, friend and most importantly a servant of The Most High God! In addition, Jill is a Life Coach, bible teacher, conference speaker, prayer intercessor and a new author. Jill holds a Masters Degree from Pepperdine University in psychology and is currently a Doctoral Candidate for her PhD in psychology from Grand Canyon University. Jill currently works as a Supervisor for a non-profit organization in Los Angeles County.

Jill's passion is to encourage and inspire women everywhere to live their best lives and to be all that God created them to be. Her mission in life is to teach women how to live beyond boarders and to go beyond limits. Is there anything too hard for God?

For speaking engagements, Jill can be reached at jillelam13@gmail.com.

HOW I WENT FROM A GED TO A PhD

by Jill Elam

My mother often shares a story of when I was five years old, I ordered something from an ad in a magazine and at the time, she didn't know that I could read. Ok I'll tell what I ordered; it was some quick hair growing grease, it never worked and I'm still searching until this day for that product to grow my hair quick. The reason I tell that story is because I've always been academically inclined. From a very young age, education came easy for me. However, through several childhood experiences I became distracted and uninterested until one day, God!

I have many stories I could share but the reason I chose this one is because, like many women out there, I waited a longtime to start chasing my dreams. As a young girl, I was very bright. I started school at four years old and even then I was ahead of my class. Twice, it was recommended that I skip a grade. How does a girl with so much academic promise drop out of high school and end up with a GED?

I share my story to hopefully inspire other women: — not just follow their dreams but chase their dreams. We've all heard the saying, "Nothing comes to a sleeper, but a dream" and it's true that nothing will happen until we take action. Having a good plan means nothing without execution. You will face challenges while pursuing your dreams, however, you must push through every obstacle you encounter.

Growing up I was a daddy's girl. I was the baby until my younger sister and brother were born. My dad and I took road trips together, just us two. I was the closest to my dad out of all my siblings. Life was perfect until the day I realized my friend and protector would no longer be around. My father didn't pass away, but it felt that way. My parents split up and my safe and secure home was pulled from under me. I didn't have my father with me every day. I went from feeling loved and secure to feeling unwanted and abandoned. Once the doorway to abandonment opens, it breeds all types of insecurities. I went from a fun, loving kid to a juvenile delinquent. From the 8th grade until 12th grade, I attended eleven junior high and high schools. I was kicked out of the entire Los Angeles School District system so my mother paid for me to attend a private Catholic school. My mother was later informed that I was expelled from Catholic school because I was failing all of my classes, smoking marijuana, drinking and hanging out with the wrong crowd.

By this time, I had no fear and my mother sent me to live with my father. It was too late. I was on the wrong track. Lightweight drugs lead me to hardcore drugs. By the age of sixteen, I was involved in drug deals, gang violence and witnessed murders. Most of the people I knew during that time of my life are now dead or in prison. I lived this lifestyle for many years and the majority of my friends were drug dealers, which meant I got free drugs but many were being killed or going to prison. Yet, I loved my life. I loved doing what I wanted to do – drugs, alcohol and fighting. I felt invincible, carrying a gun and talking big. Unfortunately, the anger and fighting carried over into my adult life. After many years of self-abuse; God rescued me!

At twenty-six years old, I ran into a good friend who committed her life to the Lord. She invited me to her church for a revival and my life changed that night. I dedicated my life to Christ and haven't looked back. God is real. He took a broken girl with a lot of holes and made her whole. Some things He delivered me from right away, but other things were a process. After accepting Christ, I thought life would be smooth sailing but it wasn't. My brother was killed and my father was diagnosed with Leukemia. My faith was being tested, but God carried me through. My father survived, but the treatment was mentally and physically taxing. I had to now become the caregiver for the one who cared for me my whole life. As hard as it was to watch my father go through all these horrible side effects my faith in God grew daily.

I went from high school drop out with a GED to a PhD when God reignited my passion for academics. I've always had a desire to go back to school but, life just keep getting in the way. I can remember sitting at a graduation, listening to them call the names of all the graduates thinking, I wish that was my name they were calling, and right then and there this feeling came over me, and I remember thinking that could be your name they call one day.

Once I saw it, I believed it. Believing you can is half the battle. The bible tells us in John 10:10, the thief's purpose is to steal and kill and destroy. My (Jesus) purpose is to give them a rich and satisfying life. So when the enemy begins to speak lies to you about how you can't do this or that; remember he's a liar and the father of lies and that Jesus came for us to live in abundance. Abundant joy, peace, health wealth, success, happy marriages and anything else you can ask or think.

My sister teases me and calls me a professional student, as I keep going back for various degrees. When I think about that, I laugh because it is true. I love education. It's a part of my purpose. Knowing what your purpose in life is and or what you are gifted in is half the battle. Your goals and dreams may be completely different from mine, only you know what that is however, remember it won't happen overnight, it may take years of work. Anything you do in life that is meaningful will require you to make sacrifices of time, family, money and emotional exhaustion. If I were truly honest, there were times when I wanted to give up and quit, especially after my brother was killed. But I remembered what one of my favorite pastors used to say, "Winners never quit and quitters never win." That little saying kept me going in those hard times. Like me, you too will face hard times, but just keep moving forward, it will be worth it in the end.

In my thirties, I went back to school while working a full time job, doing ministry and maintaining family relationships. I earned an associate degree and transferred to a university to earn an undergraduate degree. I continued on to graduate school, earning a graduate degree from Pepperdine University. I had no intentions on earning a doctoral degree at fifty years old but God had other plans for me.

You are not too old to go after your dreams. It is not too late! I started college in my thirties and will finally complete my doctoral degree at the age of fifty. You know they say 50 is the new 30, I'll take that. When I counsel women, I hear so many excuses as to why they are stuck and can't move forward. Excuses are just that: excuses. Be determined to live your best life and go after those dreams and goals that are God given. There is nothing like walking in purpose. I challenge you to live in purpose and live on purpose.

Lastly, I've always had a desire to be married. After walking with the Lord for twenty years and watching other women get married, God blessed me with a husband at the age of forty-seven. I have often felt like a late bloomer, but I will tell you, it's better to bloom late than never bloom at all. If I can do it, you can do it too. If you don't remember anything else about my story, please remember it's never too late to pursue your dreams. I pray that my story encourages you to chase your dreams, to hold on and never ever give up.

Every challenge and obstacle is defeated one decision at a time. It has been asked; how do you eat an elephant? The answer is simple, one bite at a time. Don't let thoughts like I'm too old, I'm not smart enough or I don't have time be a barrier between you and your dreams. I'm no smarter than you, no less busy than you, and yet somehow I've managed to go from GED to a PhD.

Listen, time is going to pass, next year will come, the question is, will you be in the same spot this time next year or will you have taken steps towards fulfilling your dreams and goals.

Before and during my educational journey and life in general, there are affirmations I use to encourage myself along the way, I want to share a few with you:

1. I was created for greatness; I am great, in God!

2. Yes, I am different, but that's just what the creator ordered!

3. I refuse to play small!

4. I reject any and all negative words that try to distract me!

5. Inhale faith, exhale fear!

6. Pray or worry, but you can't do both! Either you trust God or you don't!

7. Last but not least, my favorite scripture; "I can do all things through Christ who strengthens me!" (Philippians 4:13).

Blessings of hope, my sister, from a little girl from a broken home who dropped out of school and choose a drug and crime ridden existence over her dreams until the loving hand of God reached in, pulled her out and gave her another chance. In pop culture, there is a term YOLO meaning you only live once. Embrace your God given talents and use them to create the life you want. I hope you are inspired to live out loud for the Lord. YOLO!

Daily prayer:

Holy and great God, I submit myself to you today. Forgive me of any and all sin, known and unknown. Create in me a clean heart and renew your right spirit within me. Use me for your glory and let my light shine bright today. Bless me to be a blessing to others. I command this day to be great! Lord your word declares that you came that I would have life and have it in abundance. I receive your abundance; I receive your grace and your mercy that is new every morning. Because of your shed blood, I am an overcomer. I know with you, I can do all things and that nothing is too hard for you! This is the day that The Lord has made I will rejoice and be glad in it! I give you thanks and praise that my dreams will flourish and all of my plans will succeed. My future is bright and everything I need you will supply! I pray this prayer in the name that is above every name, in the strong and mighty name of Jesus, Amen and Amen!

Teecha Chamblee

Teecha Chamblee, known to many as Ms. Tee, is the CEO of Ms. Tee Family Daycare and Home Decorating Solutions. The mother to three wonderful children, Ms. Tee is known for her hard work, loving heart, organization skills, and commitment to her goals. As a woman of God, Ms. Tee has dedicated her life to serving God, and has made it her mission to bring her family, friends, and other loved ones to the Lord.

Teecha Chamblee was born in New Orleans, Louisiana but grew up in Cerritos, California. She attended Cerritos College, completing her Associates of Arts Degree in General Studies, with an emphasis on Early Childhood Education. She holds a Bachelor of Science Degree in Business Management, a Master of Health Administration Degree, and an Interior Decorator Diploma. She worked as a Preschool Teacher for seven years, and has dedicated her life to helping others working in health care management for 11 years. She currently resides in Lake Elsinore, California.

Connect with Ms. Tee on Facebook or at teechacc@gmail.com, or msteefamilydaycare@gmail.com.

LOVING THE NEW ME

by Teecha Chamblee

I was lying down on the bed, being rolled down the hallway. He seemed to be pushing me rather fast. Everything was so bright. The walls were white and plain. The man pushed me through the double doors. When we entered the doors, there was this really big and tall Black man that greeted me. I grabbed his hand and said, "Please don't let me die, please don't let me die." He said, "I won't let anything happen to you. I'm going to push some medicine in here and I want you to count to 10 with me." We started counting. One, two, three......Everything went dark.

I looked to my left. I looked to my right. There were so many strange faces all around me and it was so loud. People were laughing and screaming with excitement. There were toddlers crying, parents yelling, and people screaming. Everyone was having a great time except for me.

h spacingIt was Friday, April 21, 2006, and my family and I were visiting Disneyland's California Adventure. I was sitting on a bench near the one of the rides, waiting for my husband and kids to get off of a ride when I suddenly felt sick. I was light-headed, dizzy, and nauseous. I felt like I was too weak to stand on my own feet. As soon as I saw my family, I told my husband that something was wrong with me and that we need to get to urgent care immediately.

We left the park and headed to urgent care. The 25 minute ride from Anaheim, California to Downey, California seemed to take forever. I was so dizzy and nauseous and had the worst headache ever. The doctor asked me if I had been out of the country. I told him no, that I had never been out of the country. He said I had a nasty virus and a 101 degrees temperature and that I would just have to "ride it out." He advised me to get plenty of rest, drink lots of fluids, and to follow-up with my primary care doctor on Monday if the symptoms worsened over the weekend. Little did I know that this virus would last the next 10 months.

By Monday morning, as they say, I was "sick as a dog." I walked into my doctor's office with a 103.5 degree fever. I told her, "I am sick."

She looked at me and said, "Not again. We just got you over chronic anemia a few months ago." She asked me had I been out of the country. I told her I had never been out of the country. She gave me some medication and told me to return if the symptoms continued. I took the medication twice and noticed my joints begin to stiffen. I literally could not move. I went to the ER. I was told that I had a reaction to the medication, stiffening of the joints, and to stop taking it immediately. I was sent back home after one bag of intravenous (IV) fluid and pain medication and told to return if the symptoms continued.

My fever returned resulting in another trip to the ER. The doctor told my family that I would need a spinal tap procedure and some blood cultures. I was not sure what these tests were. According to WebMD, "A spinal tap or a lumbar puncture is a medical test in which fluid is collected from an area surrounding the spinal cord. The sample is studied for traces of bacteria and other infectious agents and is tested for blood cell count, protein, and other blood components. This test can be used to diagnose meningitis, MS, cancer, and more. A blood culture is a test to find an infection in the blood. The blood does not normally have any bacteria or fungi in it. A blood culture can show what bacteria or fungi are in the blood."

The doctor tried to make light of the situation by making a joke, but there was nothing funny at the time. He gave me IV fluid with the pain medication, morphine, to ease my pain and to help me relax. He told my family that he had performed thousands of spinal tap procedures. It should be quick and simple and he would find out what was wrong with me. He prepped the space on my back and had me lay on my side. He said I would feel something cold and a lot of pressure. He had a nurse hug me so I would not move. I tried to remain still but when the needle entered

116

my back, my natural reflexes made me jump. He wiggled the long needle around and said he could not find the space to withdraw fluid. So he pulled the needle out of my back. He apologized and said he needed to try it again. The morphine was wearing off and I could feel more than just cold and some pressure. As he wiggled it around, tears rolled down my face. He was becoming frustrated with himself and that is when I saw blood all on the floor and panicked. He apologized and cleaned my back and said that radiology would take me to have the procedure done. He put something in my IV that caused me to fall asleep and when I woke up the procedure had been finished. The spinal tap sample returned normal.

After spending hours in the ER, on June 4, 2006, I was sent home very sick. My doctors told my family that there was nothing else they could do for me. I was very sick and they could not find the problem. I told my mother to please have the pastor come and pray over me. I was too weak and exhausted and in too much pain to continue to fight this thing anymore. I asked God numerous times to please take me home. I was happy with the life I had lived so far and ready to move on. My mother's friend, a pastor, came over to pray with me. He prophesied that this was not the end for me. He said something was going on in my house and I should leave. So that evening my family grabbed a few items for me and the kids and I went to live at my parent's house for a while.

On June 6, 2006, I woke up with a large, painful lump on the right side of my neck and a 105 degrees temperature. My family called my doctor. She wanted to see me right away. When she saw me, she called the hospital to have me admitted. Once I was admitted into the hospital all three of my doctors came to look at me and the lump on my neck. They all agreed that the lump should be removed as soon as possible. They did not recommend any other course of treatment. I had no time to think about it or consider my options. I was told to remove all jewelry and to get ready for surgery. I told my mother I do not think I am going to make it through this surgery. I asked her to please take care of my two kids and let them know I love them so much. My surgery was scheduled for the next day so I went to sleep that night, in the hospital all alone and scared. I prayed and talked to God a long time that night. It was just me and Him.

On the morning of June 7, 2006, I was getting ready to have a lumpectomy on the right side of my neck when my family returned to the hospital. I was crying telling them how nervous I was. I was scared to death. I had never had surgery before. My aunt stepped out of the room while I was crying and came back with a tiny cross. She told me to hold it and we prayed. My aunt from Mississippi called me and reminded me that John 11:4 says, "When Jesus heard that, he said, This sickness is not unto death, but for the glory of God, that the Son of God might be glorified

118

thereby." My mother began reciting Psalm 23:4, "Yea, though I walk through the valley of the shadow of death, I will fear no evil: for thou art with me; thy rod and thy staff they comfort me." She told me to repeat it to comfort myself so I repeated it several times. The nurse came in my room to take me to the operating room. He rolled my bed down a few long hallways. We seemed to be going rather fast. Everything was so bright. The walls were white and plain. He pushed me through the double doors. We entered the doors and approached a really big and tall African man. He introduced himself as the anesthesiologist. I grabbed his hand and said, "Please don't let me die. Please don't let me die." He said, "I won't let anything happen to you. I'm going to push some medicine in here and I want you to count to ten with me." We started counting. One, two, three......Everything went dark.

I finally woke up. I was disoriented. I forgot where I was for a moment. I tried to swallow and couldn't. The nurse came in and said the surgery went well. I told her my throat hurt. She said because a camera was put down my throat during surgery. She took me back to my room where my family was waiting and ready to see me. I was so happy to see them as well. I cried like a baby again.

This was just the beginning to my long road of recovery. I was going home with a strong cancer-type of medication that goes directly into your blood stream and kills everything in the body, both good and bad cells. The medication was given intravenously only for the next few months. My veins had become so weakened from all of the blood draws and cultures, that they could not withstand being punctured anymore. That meant I would be going home with a PICC line inserted into my central vein. I did not like this idea, but if it was going to help me recover faster, I was willing to give it a try. The simple procedure of inserting a PICC line was not so simple. I did not realize I was going to be awake for the procedure.

I was finally released from the hospital. However, being home proved to be more nerve-wrecking than I anticipated. I still had a high fever, but it was stable. I hated looking at the PICC line with the two catheters hanging from my left arm; one to insert the medication; the other for the home health nurse to stop by daily and take blood. I was still haunted by the images of the PICC line procedure. I was very uncomfortable lying down on my left side where the PICC line was. I felt every time I moved I was going to puncture my heart. I could still see the vivid images of the needle going in my arm and all the way up to my heart. I could still see my heart beat. After about a week of struggling with the PICC line I requested for it to be removed. Naturally, this slowed down my recovery progress because I had to change the medication I was taking to a pill form instead of the IV form. I was okay with that.

A few weeks later I saw my primary care doctor. She informed me that the pathology report came back and found thousands of tiny abscesses, or infections, in the mass that were causing the fever. They do not know what caused the abscesses, since infection was never found. I was diagnosed as fever with unknown origin, whatever that means.

As the weeks went by, I slowly regained my strength and energy. I was encouraged to have a blood transfusion but my hemoglobin levels improved with the use of iron supplements and weekly B-12 shots. My fever decreased each day. My appetite returned and I gained a few pounds. My school granted me a disability status and I was able to complete homework and papers at my own pace so I decided to return to school to finish my last few weeks. The illness forced me to take a leave of absence from two courses, 12 weeks. I was unable to graduate in June with the group I started with but I graduated later in September.

January 2007, I found out that I was expecting a baby. Pregnant— Seriously? We had become distant during my illness but my husband and I had started spending time together again once I got better.

I went to see my OB/GYN and indirectly she explained the risks that I could be taking with my own health if I continued the pregnancy and how high the chances of having an unhealthy baby were because of the medication I had been taking the past several months. I had to talk this over with God. There was no way I was going to discuss this with my family and friends, after the ordeal I had just experienced. After careful consideration of the situation and many nights of prayer, I decided to continue the pregnancy.

The pregnancy started off good considering that I was high risk. The pregnancy was progressing well until I was 18 weeks pregnant. I began spotting and cramping and after a few visits to the ER and my OB/GYN, I was taken off of work at 20 weeks. My family was well-aware of my pregnancy by then and surprisingly excited about the new arrival. Praise God, I delivered a healthy baby boy in September 2007. The labor was long, intense, and exhausting and took a huge toll on my already weakened body.

Shortly after the delivery, my body began to get weaker and I was experiencing frequent joint and muscle pain. There were times I was so stiff and in so much pain that I was unable to pick up the baby when he cried. I went back to my primary care doctor. She could not diagnose me with any particular condition, so she sent me to a rheumatologist.

After 11 months of testing and drugs, in August 2008, he diagnosed me with Mixed Connective Tissue Disease (MCTD). MTCD is a rare connective tissue disorder. MCTD is used to describe what may be an overlapping group of connective tissue disorders that cannot be diagnosed in more specific terms. These disorders include Systemic Lupus Erythematosus, Polymyositis, and Scleroderma. Individuals with MCTD have symptoms of each of these disorders including arthritis, cardiac and pulmonary issues, skin manifestations, kidney disease, muscle weakness, and dysfunction of the esophagus. The exact cause of Mixed Connective Tissue Disease is unknown. He said that he would be treating me as a Lupus patient. He started me on several medications and I began taking them immediately, not knowing the severity of the diseases or medications.

Within a month of taking the medications, I gained an excessive amount of weight. People that knew me well would ask me what was wrong with me. I wore a size 4/6 at the time I became ill. None of my clothes fit. I was taking about 13 pills every day. One of the medications caused me to get hard, painful lumps in the back of my head. Another caused my hair to thin and fall out in clumps. Another medication affected my vision so I had to have my pupils dilated annually. Taking so many medications gave me dry eye and dry mouth. I stopped wearing contacts because my eyes would get so dry. The medication for dry mouth made me drool. I was always out of breath. I had rolls of fat that I never had before. I developed high blood pressure. I quickly fell into a mild state of depression. It was going to take me some time to get used to wearing a size 16. Even I had to stare at the new round face in the mirror and ask myself who is this new person.

Since my diagnosis I have been hospitalized several times. I recall being in the hospital one night and waking up because I lost feeling in my feet. I pulled my blankets up and noticed that my feet had lost their color. They were all white and pale on the bottom. My hands were the same way. I freaked out. I just knew I was dead. I woke up my aunt, who had stayed in the hospital with me that night. She confirmed that I definitely was not dead but something was certainly wrong with my hands and feet. She called the nurse to come check on me. The nurse looked at my feet and hands and left to get the doctor. She returned with the doctor and about five or six more nurses. They looked at my feet and hands and were so excited. I was still nervous and freaking out, not understanding what the excitement was about. The doctor said it looked like I had Raynaud's Phenomenon and they were excited because they had never seen it on a patient before. I had never heard of it before. The doctor told the nurse to bring extra blankets and cover me up. She said I would be fine and that I needed to warm up my body. It took a few days for the color to completely return and it still happens whenever I get very cold.

Many times I have minor illnesses in which my body attacks itself and I am not aware that I am sick until the illness is severe. I have joint pain on a regular basis. My iron, potassium, and magnesium levels remain low. I currently take seven pills daily, instead of 13, and a few supplements. Each year the disease progresses and I have a new symptom. The illness causes allergies and rashes as well. However, I visit my doctor every three months, take my medications as prescribed, and have my blood drawn regularly to check my kidneys and other vital organs that the disease affects. Each day is different. Some days, life is normal and I can perform daily functions fairly easy. Some days are difficult and just getting out of my bed is a challenge. Regardless of how I feel, every day that I can open my eyes and be in my right mind is a blessing.

I used to ask God, why me? What did I do to deserve all that I went through? There were so many days that I wanted to give up. I did not think I could live the rest of my life like this. I had three children to support and I did not have the strength or energy to be bothered with them. I did not know how I was going to live a life in daily pain.

Before the surgery, I used to wake up every morning and listen to Smokie Norful's version of "God is Able." I would play it over and over again and just talk to God and it finally hit me that I need to truly trust God because He is truly able.

If we never go through anything, how can we tell others about how great God is? How can we testify and truly believe what we are sharing with others if we do not have anything to share? God uses our lives as an example to others. He tests our faith at times to see if we truly believe in Him. Not only do we need the will to continue on, or the desire to succeed, but we also need to trust in God and His plan for our lives. God knows what He is doing. He knew where I was and where He wanted me to be. He never left me during this entire ordeal.

I earned a Master's degree in 2011. I purchased my first home in 2012 and recently opened a home daycare in April of 2016. I thank God for His grace and favor. I may be a new person physically, with challenges and limitations, but I am who God wants me to be. I am loving the new me. I share my story with you in hopes of giving you encouragement if you are going through a situation that you do not think you can get out of. Trust God. Pray. Stay in the word of God. He will see you through. He is able.

Lateisha Johnson

Lateisha is a wonderful person with a big heart and a beautiful smile. She loves helping others. She is proud to say that she is a twin sister. Not only that, but she has other siblings who are also twins.

Lateisha has accomplished a lot in her life. After graduating from Quartz Hills High school in 2006, she graduated from Antelope Valley Medical School and studied billing and coding. She received her Billing and

Coding Certificate in 2007. Lateisha, wanted to go back to school for business and she did just that. She attended Mt. San Jacinto Community College and finished business class in 2010.

Because she is gifted at doing hair, Lateisha felt the need to go to cosmetology school. She successfully completed cosmetology school and received her diploma from Marinello School of Beauty in Hemet, Ca. in 2012. There is nothing that Lateisha can't do when she puts her mind to it. Although she has gone through bad relationships and suffered many ups and downs, she is a true witness of perseverance and hard work. She tells everyone she comes in contact with to go after your dreams. She believes there is a light at the end of the tunnel if you don't give up.

THE LIFE BEHIND ME

by Lateisha Johnson

My name is Lateisha Johnson. I'm from Compton, California. My mother had 7 children including two sets of twins. I have 5 sisters and 1 brother. My twin sister, Keisha, and I were born two minutes apart. My mother was murdered in front of me when I was 3 years old in a drive by shooting. She was shot in the head in front of my auntie's house. That was 1992.

My grandmother took me and my sisters into her home in Lancaster, California. She treated us like we were her own and always told us that we were her babies; nobody would be able to come between us. She was from Houston, Texas and she didn't take mess from nobody. You couldn't get over on her because she already new the game and she would tell you, "I been to school, I know the rules. I ain't no fool."

Granny was funny and sweet. She would give her all just to help someone else out and always made a way, for me and my sister, family and friends. We didn't have a lot growing up but Granny made a way.

Granny got sick while I was in high school. I took care of her. When I started to notice Granny was forgetting things little by little, she had to stop cooking, and I started cooking for us all the time. There were five people in the house then: me, my twin, Keisha, our little sister, Ro-Ro, our uncle and Granny.

Sometimes Granny didn't have money for school clothes or school stuff, so I started stealing out if the stores, so Keisha, Ro-Ro and Granny and I would be all right. I would steal clothes and shoes for my sisters so they could have them for school. I would steal soap and tissue for the house. I made sure my sister was all right and I made sure my granny was all right. I made sure we had food, and house supplies but I had remind Granny to pay the rent and bills because she would forget. Some Christmases we didn't get any gifts; we barely had food. When I was 15 I stopped stealing and got a job through the work program at school.

One day Keisha, Ro-Ro and I went to our cousin's grandmother's house to wash our clothes and she never took us back home. She called CPS on my granny and told them Granny was beating us, we didn't have food, and my uncle was a drunk. I was so mad. CPS didn't want us to go back home. Weeks later our cousin's grandmother got custody of us. My sister and I cried and cried. We were so mad that we were in the system with our cousins. There was a total of six of us; three of my cousins, Keisha, Ro-Ro and I all under one roof. Their mother had a real bad drinking problem and were taken when they were a babies.

Granny got really depressed. We were all she had. It was sad enough that she was forgetting things, losing us didn't make the situation any better. We were told by the court we could only go see our Granny with our cousin's grandmother. We couldn't go see her by our selves. I was mad. My sister was crying. I wasn't crying though because nothing was going to stop me from seeing my Granny, she was the only mother I knew.

I was my Granny's help and I was so worried about whether she ate and if she took her medication. I skipped school and called out from work to go see her. I would take her food and house supplies and spend time with her. I wanted to make sure she was all right. Sometimes she would give me a list to go to the store. I didn't have a car so I would push the basket back with everything she wanted. My uncle was a drunk, he was always drunk, so he couldn't help.

Granny was always happy to see me. She was my mother, my friend, my grandmother, my father, she was my everything and I was willing to do anything for her. I didn't care what the courts said, that was my mom. I didn't care if I became broke helping her, I would use one paycheck to buy shoes and clothes and the other one I would help my Granny. It wasn't a lot but it was something,

When you are 15 and in high school, they only you only allow to work a certain number of hours but I did the best I could by myself. Sometimes my Granny would say don't worry about her, she was fine, just focus on school and save my money, but I couldn't just focus on my self. That would have been selfish, which Im not.

I'm selfless and had always put my family ahead of me— my Granny, Keisha, Ro-Ro, and my uncle.

I got pregnant at the age of 16. I was so scared to tell Granny. I was worried so I was going to get my cousin to tell her. Before she could I went over to visit Granny and she was like, "You pregnant?"

I just looked at her, I didn't know what to say, she asked me again and I said, "Yeah, I'm so sorry, Granny. Are you mad at me?" She said no, she was mad that I didn't tell her. She already knew. She told me to stay in school don't drop out because I was going to make it in life and she didn't want me to be like my older sister in the street living that life.

I asked her how she knew. She said, "A mother always no her child." She gave me a hug and a kiss and told me she loved me. I told her I was going to make her proud of me and I would finish everything I start.

A month later Granny lost her apartment and went to live with my auntie in Compton. I had lost my baby around the same time. The doctors said I wasn't eating and my stress level was high. I was so sad because I wanted my baby but I was still young and in high school. The child's father was cheating and already had one baby and another on the way. All three of us were pregnant at the same time, so he was going to have 3 kids. I didn't know he was cheating until I lost my baby.

A month went by and Granny's health didn't get any better. She had her toe cut off. She was Diabetic and had

Alzheimer's. She couldn't remember recent things, but she could remember 40 years back.

I had been placed in a group home when I got pregnant, but after I lost my baby they still kept me there. I was in the group home a whole year, but that didn't stop me from seeing my Granny. I had home passes: that's what they called it when you get to go home on the weekend or a holiday. The group home was in North Hill, California so the staff would drive me two hours to my auntie's house in Compton to see Granny. I was able to visit with my auntie, Granny, my cousin, Cherry, Keisha, Ro-Ro, and my cousin's grandmother. I looked forward to weekend visits but sometimes I couldn't go home. I would just be at the group home with the other girls.

The group home was a private boarding school. We were not allowed to bring anything to the school, no backpack, no food, no paper, nothing. They had everything at the school. I used to sneak food in. I didn't like their food, I only liked the junk food, chips, juice, and cookies.

I felt so sad in the home. I felt like nobody cared about me. Keisha and Ro-Ro, my cousin's grandmother and my little cousin that lived with her came to visit only every once in a while but I was grateful that they did come to see me. I felt like I was in jail. We couldn't go anywhere without the staff. The staff took us places so we wouldn't be in the house all the time. You could only go if you were on good level. They had levels A, B, C, and R. R level is bad. It meant you couldn't go anywhere, not even on home pass. I was on level B.

When we went out everybody knew we were in a group home because we all went as a group, but not me, I always stood out. I didn't act my age and I would always walk ahead of them because I didn't want anybody to know I was in a group home. As time went by I didn't care any more and my focus was getting out of there and making money. I would do the other girls' hair, and they would pay me $20 a week. I used to save that so when I went home I would have money. I was so determined to go home all I could think about was my sisters and brother and my Granny.

I went back to my cousin's grandmother's house in August 2005. I went back to public school. I didn't want to get in any trouble so I asked if I could be placed on Independent Study for which I only had to go once a week. It was my last year in high school. I used to pay my sister Ro-Ro to do my homework and I would go take my tests and pass. I was done with all my testing and school by the end of February 2006.

My teacher told me to come back in June for the graduation walk. I was so happy. I had four months to kill so I got me another job and got enrolled into college. I took classes until it was time to graduate from high school.

I had 10 tickets for graduation. I had two for my auntie and my Granny to come but Granny couldn't make it. Auntie said my Granny wasn't going to be able to sit there. I was so hurt. Out of all the people in the world, I wanted her to come. Ro-Ro and Keisha came and two of my cousins and my auntie, the one who said I would never graduate and that she didn't like me. She came and brought a gift.

I showed everyone who told me I wasn't going make it. Even after all I had been through I graduated on time. There were 800 kids in my graduating class. It was the largest class in all of Los Angels County at that time. I was so happy I did it. I made my Granny proud of me and I know my mother was looking down on me from heaven. I was the first one of her kids to finish school. I made my Granny a copy of my diploma, put it in a frame and gave it to her. She was happy.

After high school I went to medical school and graduated with a Medical Billing Certificate. I moved out with my boyfriend. He and I and got our own place in Hemet, California.

I really loved this man and cared about him. Our families grew up together and he made me happy. I thought I knew him but I really didn't. I would come home from school and he would be really mad at me. I didn't understand why he was so mad all the time. He would beat me, rip my clothes off, call me all kind of names, and ask why did I think I was better than him. I didn't think I was better than anybody. I just wanted the best for my life, that's why I stayed in school. Soon as I got done with one class I enrolled in another.

He didn't like me going to school. He didn't like me going to church. He would even tell me he didn't love me and that he was just using me. He told me the reason why he left marks on my face was because he wanted other men to see I wasn't cute anymore. He said if he left marks nobody would want me. I tried to leave but he would stop me or he would find me and tell me if I ever left him again he would kill me. He slept with a knife under the bed to make sure I didn't try to leave. It was really hard trying to leave him when he kept saying he would kill me .

I changed all my classes so he wouldn't check on me or try to enroll into my classes, but somehow he found out and enrolled himself into my classes so he could watch me. He thought I was sleeping with everyone in the class. He didn't trust me. He would always say I wouldn't make it without him. Eventually he went to jail because he beat me so bad. I had black eyes, marks on my body, my body hurt from fighting, and I had cuts on my face and body.

I couldn't take it any more. I cried out for help and prayed. The next day I found out I had an uncle that lived close by. My auntie gave me his number and told me to call him, he might be able to help me. I called him and asked him to come get me. I was crying. I never called my family to ask for anything, but I needed to be around family. I needed love.

When I left I just took all my clothes. I was sad and afraid. My uncle and aunt prayed for me and allowed me to stay in their home. I slept in the oldest daughter's room.

My auntie even let me borrow some money to get to school on the bus but I didn't stay long.

When my boyfriend got out of jail and said he wasn't going to hit me any more and that he was sorry, he came and got me. The next day when I received my paycheck I cashed it and took the money back and put it on the table at my uncle and aunt's house and thanked them for letting me stay.

My auntie called from Los Angeles and asked me where I was. I told her I left and went back home. I told her my boyfriend came and got me. She told me to be careful because he would do it again and that they loved me. Not even 4 days he was back at hitting me and calling me names again. I would fight back but it wasn't helping. I would take fast showers because I would have to watch my back just in case he tried to do something to me in the shower. I never took a bath with a tub full of water because I thought he would drown me and kill me. I aways kept the shower curtain open so I could see when he was coming. He was always around. He didn't work. He had a heart problem. He got a disability check and I was his care giver.

One day he started tripping, he called me out of my name. He told me how he got another girl pregnant and how he didn't love me, he didn't care, and how nobody wanted me. I couldn't take it any more. I got tired of him putting his hands on me. I went into the kitchen, grabbed a butter knife and tried to cut him with it. I missed him and hit the refrigerator and cut my two of my own fingers. I was so much in pain. The flesh of my hand was hanging. He tried to help me. I didn't want him touching me but I knew I had to go to the emergency room and I couldn't drive, so he took me. I had to get stitches. In one finger I got five stitches and in the other I got eight. He didn't say anything bad to me or try to hit me until after a month when I got the stitches out. Then he started all over again. I was feed up. I called my friend, put all my stuff out side and she came and got me. She helped me get all my stuff out.

He was mad. He called the police. They came and it was the same police who took him to jail the first time. The police looked at me, laughed and said take everything don't leave nothing behind. He said he couldn't do anything because I already had my stuff out side. He told me never to come back. I took all my stuff and never looked back.

My grandmother passed away in 2011. That was the hardest thing in my life to deal with. I missed school and I didn't think I was going to graduate, but I did and my uncle and aunt came, two of my sisters and some other people I didn't know.

I was told by my big cousin and by my Granny never to let anything stop me and I haven't. My new boyfriend and I moved out of California to Phoenix, Arizona. We moved to a 2 bedroom 2 bath apartment. Not only did I get myself a job I got my boyfriend a job also. He was cheating on me. He told me, and I believed he was going to get it together once we moved to Arizona but I was wrong and I felt so stupid for taking him back. He was cheating with a girl that was only 17 years old. She dropped out of school just to be with him.

When I found out I told the little girl I new about her and him. She said, "So." I just laughed and told her he would do her the same way. She said, "No he's not because we're in love." We were in the break room at work. I told her she was only 17 having sex with him and he is 29. She said yes she was. So? Did I want to smell her private part? I got up and slapped her. I felt very disrespected. I was so hurt that he did that to me. Everybody knew about them at the job except me. I did not think he would be sleeping with a little girl. I was so hurt that day, and, I was fired for slapping her. Everybody at the job knew. They talked about it but they didn't tell me anything. I remember one of my coworkers held me while I cried. He was the only one who showed any sympathy, he was the only one who told me it would be all right. Two months later I got a job working at the Western Kirkland Resort and Spa Hotel in Scottsdale, Arizona.

Once I broke up with my boyfriend for good I got an even better job working with disabled people in a group home. I moved into a 3 bedroom house. It has been years since then and haven't talked to or seen anybody from my past. I came a long way in life. I had to grow up early and I had to learn how to apply what I learned to my life. Through it all God saved me. I thank Him for all of my blessings. I learned to put God first in life and because of that, I'm stronger.

I built what people said I could not build, I walked where people said I could not walk, I have done everything I said I was going to do. I'm currently dating a man who thinks so much of me and who's not putting his hands on me. I pray God will bless us as we take it step-by-step. I trust the plans God has for us. My life is in His hands.

Tara L. Culton

Tara Culton is a 21st Century Visionairre. Her unique gifts and her calling has helped many in the Body of Christ and other arenas. Those who have experienced her ministry and know her best call her the "Vision Fixer." Bring her your ideas and your vision and she will help you execute excellence. Her life experiences have taught her "An idea is cheap: Execution is priceless."

Tara has been in ministry for many years. She is an ordained Elder set in the office of Teacher. She is a prophetic psalmist, minister of flags, administrator, speaker, teacher, and author. She is the founder of All For Worship Ministries, TLC Kingdom Expressions, OnTime Tasks, and the Co-Founder of Priestly Worship Ministries. She can be reached at info@taraculton.com or via phone at 804-252-4735.

DISCIPLED IN DEPRESSION

"Mental Illness. It's a disease…NOT a shame."

– Tara L. Culton

Lord, Jesus! What day is it? Sunday? Geez! Church time. Time to assemble myself together with other disciples. But, wait. My body aches. My head hurts. My chest is tighter than a stretched rubber band. I'm totally exhausted! And, you want me to get up and go to church?! I can't do it. I just can't.

I was preparing for a move. A move that was supposed to take place in a few days. Not <u>that</u> day. My mind's refrain was, "How am I going to get all of this done?" Nevertheless, there I stood one Saturday night in the pouring rain, with my asthmatic self, loading a truck at 9:00 pm! I was beside myself and didn't even know how to spell exhaustion. Just two days after that, my sisters told me that my mother, who lives in a different state, was gravely ill and that I should come home as soon as possible.

WHAT? I'm barely moving due to extreme fatigue. I have no leave on my job to make this trip possible and I don't have the finances for it either. "Jesus, no more!" I screamed. I tried making sense of it all. Instead, I found myself sitting on the floor of my room, surrounded by unpacked boxes, thoroughly drained, and staring off in space. I pleaded, "PLEASE, Lord, make it stop. I can't handle another thing right now." But it didn't stop. Two days, for real, two days after hearing about my mother, the doctors told me I had a blood clot. "Really? *This* is how it's going down, Lord? You're kidding me, right?!"

Have you ever been in that place? The place where the world seems to come crashing in on you all at once? To put it frankly, for most of my life, I have lived in that place. I could take some things in stride but for many others my mind made mountains out of mole hills. From my vantage point, everything was important. Everything was urgent. I believed it was my job to make it all happen. I lived in a place of racing thoughts and conflicting behaviors. In short, I fought with mental illness and its aftermath. I fought hard. I needed to hide my mental health challenges, my *discipleship in depression*, though I didn't know that's what my challenges were at the time.

I fought everyone and everything. Fighting was all I knew. Do you remember this line, "All my life I had to fight?" It's from the movie, "The Color Purple?[1]" To that line, I add, I had to fight in my family, I had to fight with family friends, and I had to fight schoolmates. What I didn't know was that I had to fight in the house of the Lord.

---

[1] APA **(6th ed.)** Walker, A. (1992). The Color Purple. London: Women's Press.

God's house – the church[2]. The very place that I'm supposed to find comfort, refuge, guidance, and support was the place that held the most pain for me: The church. In the church, I fortified the thoughts, "I'm not good enough. I've got to overcompensate. I've got to take care of me because no one else will." In the church, I learned to hide. In the church, I learned to fake it. And, it was mostly in the church where my life played out like a grand TV miniseries where mental health illness was the star. I was not only being discipled as a follower of Jesus Christ but I was also being *discipled in depression.*

My mental health challenges began in my childhood. My first instructor was my father. To be sure, I was a Daddy's Girl; and, my father was my knight in shining armor. He was also a high functioning, abusive alcoholic. Although he never ever sexually assaulted me, my sisters, or anyone else, he did introduce domestic violence and other types of abuse into my life. For instance, like a lot of children in my culture, physical spankings were a part of my world. When my father was really angry, it went beyond mere spanking. His abuse was also verbal and emotional. In my opinion, I believe that stemmed from my father's inability to deal with his own pain and anger...all fueled by his alcoholism. I was often walking on eggshells to keep him happy. I never knew if

---

[2] The word 'church is a conglomeration of the various faith communities of which I've been a part.

he or his alcoholism would show up. This planted the seeds that would sprout as people-pleasing behavior later on. Even with all of this, I, like most children, adored my father. His death at age 29, (I was 9) was a pivotal event in my life. You see, no matter what my father did, he threatened to kill anyone that touched his girls. However, shortly after his death, someone did 'touch' me. With that abuse came its ride or die partners of guilt and shame.

My mother is one of 11 children born to parents with roots deep in the church. She was raised in Georgia. Her father was a pastor. Everyone knew who she was because of my grandparents' work in the ministry. I'm not sure what my mother's childhood was like. We've never really talked about it. Until recently, we had not talked about much of anything. There was much mental and emotional strain in our relationship for reasons not clear to me. When did that strain start? If I were to guess, I would say shortly after my father's death when my mother had to bury my father, relocate back to her hometown in a different state, and raise three girls alone. In my opinion, the grief of losing a husband was overwhelming for her (no matter how good or bad the relationship was). I don't know if my mother endured any childhood trauma. What I do know is that the ebb and flow of our relationship was very rocky and had a profound impact on the woman I was to become. Thank God for grace and mercy. Now, in my over fifty life space, I am so grateful that my mother and I can joke, laugh, and cry together. We truly, genuinely love each other.

My father was the oldest of 7 living siblings. He was born in a small town in Missouri to very young parents. My dad's parents were around 15 and 16 when he was born. His parents were not in the ministry; but, his paternal grandparents were. I don't know what my father's childhood was like because he died before I could have that discussion. Nonetheless, the relationship model he had in his home was that of alcoholism infused with domestic violence. Because we model what we see, my father, as I've said earlier, was an abusive alcoholic. As I look back on the short time we had together, I think I can recognize the signs of mental health illness. Whatever pain, trauma, disappointments, etc., that my father endured, he passed that on to me via physical (not sexual), emotional, and domestic abuse. Nothing, however, can compare to the abuse I would suffer after his death.

As I grew and my body developed, sexual abuse and secrecy were my normal. The abuse came at the hands of various people – both male and female. There was so much abuse of various kinds throughout my childhood and into my adult life it's mind-boggling that I'm alive to tell it. As a result of the long-term trauma, I accumulated stress, internal turmoil, and a skewed view of life in general as badges of honor. This only perpetuated the challenges of my undiagnosed mental health *dis*-ease. I just knew that everyone really knew (although I was trying to hide it) that I was having these difficulties in my thoughts and in my emotions. This was another level of my *discipleship in depression.*

Like a lot of us that experience mental health issues, I sensed something was out of balance in my thoughts and in my behaviors. I suspected that my relationships were skewed. And, I often said to myself, "Something is wrong here." But, I could not pinpoint the issue no matter how hard I tried. The truth is that even if I had known exactly what was out of place, as a child I was powerless to deal with it without proper help and support. In my case, the people that should have helped and supported me were either an instructor in my *discipleship in depression* or they were aware of the actions that created what I call "The Deeds."

My "deeds" were the mental, the physical, the emotional, and the sexual abuse of which I spoke about earlier. These things thrust me into *long-term depression discipleship*…they tainted my mental state. Like many of my counterparts who live with mental health *dis*-ease and, as I've shared with you, I was introduced to the tentacles of depression via traumatic trials and stressful situations as a child. As a result, my innocence was seized, my voice was silenced, and my mental health suffered greatly. I held distorted views about who I was and where I fit in the world. As I grew older, the distortion became evident in my thinking and in my behaviors. In my opinion, these are some of the signs of mental health illness in my life.

For a long time, I was oblivious of my mental health illness and the behaviors associated with it. These behaviors caused much pain for me both in and out of the church. And, I naïvely thought this was how God made me...lock, stock, and barrel. I thought this was who I truly was. As for the church, during my childhood, attendance at church was a requirement and it was non-negotiable. We didn't get to vote if we were going or not, there was no discussion about it. It simply was what we did. Church was an extended family of sorts. Unfortunately, this family did not provide the safety and support I needed because they either did not recognize there was a problem; recognized the problem but chose to ignore it (cultural imprint); or recognized the problem, wanted to help, but did not know how.

In my opinion, mental health illness will have you believe that you, and only you, can turn, change, or transform a situation. It will mislead you into believing that what you know to be right and to be true is not. It will trick you into questioning that gut instinct that says, "Hold on, Tara, this is not a good choice." It will dupe you into thinking that crouching down, half-naked on a back porch in cold weather is an adventure, believe me, it is not. Risky behavior is dangerous and the enemy will use those behaviors to stop you from reaching your destiny in Christ.

It will mask the places of refuge in your life. The church is one place that can serve as a refuge for those experiencing mental health illness. That is if the church would only dialogue about mental health illness and not the person.

The challenge the church faces is to be the Kingdom and not be silent. For too long the faith community has not known how or did not have the information to support those experiencing mental health illness challenges. The church has also remained silent on the matter. Historically and traditionally a person experiencing mental health illness in the church hears, "Pray harder, beef up your spiritual life, or you need deliverance." Stop it! Mental health illness is just like any other illness. Would we instruct someone to see a doctor for high blood pressure, diabetes, and asthma to name a few? Sure we would. Then why is it so challenging to view mental health *dis*-orders as another disease? Instead of concluding that a person is spiritually lacking because of mental health illness challenges, the church must talk about it (#letstalk). ***Mental health illness is a dis-ease...NOT a shame.*** Of course, we recognize that there is a spiritual component at work. However, just because someone is living with mental health illness challenges does not mean they are spiritually deficient. It also does not mean that they are their disease. What it does mean is that they need help and support in and from all areas of their life to begin a new normal.

151

My new normal is a process of *RE*-covery. *Re*-covering my mind, *re*-covering my will, and *re*-covering my emotions. It consists of accepting the fact that I was *dis*-abled in my thoughts, in my behaviors, and in my ability to handle life. I had a *dis*-abling concussion from the blows to my thoughts. The tissues of my self-worth were deeply scarred. I had broken bones from the violent emotions and behaviors. And, my self-imposed amnesia caused me to fight with flesh and blood and forget what I knew. It's not the flesh we are warring with. It's that nation of images (imagination) that we fight by casting down everything that would promote itself against God's authority. Nevertheless, because our gracious Lord knows all and He is love incarnate, He met me where I was. God is gracious and loving. His love will not allow Him to leave any one of us in despair. His desire is for us to use everything in our lives to further the Kingdom of God agenda. Everything...even mental health illness diagnoses is working for our good.

Whatever challenge or trial you may be facing, even mental health illness diagnoses, you are not alone. Furthermore, you are not your challenges or health diagnoses. Your current situation is not a predictor of your future. Your destiny is in Christ and in Him alone. If the enemy is trying to convince you that you are 'less than,' you're not. You are more than a conqueror. You are someone's blessing and they are waiting to meet you. If you feel that you've veered off course, our heavenly Father's hand can gently redirect you.

The enemy would have you believe that you are the first and the only person to ever be in your situation. Take note, that scoundrel is a liar! God is not surprised by your situation. He is not in heaven asking "How did this happen?" No. He sees the end from the beginning. The fight is fixed. We win by a landslide!

My deliverance, if you will, and my graduation from being *discipled in depression* came when I decided that where I was in my life and my mental health illness diagnoses were not my final destination. You can do that too. You can regain your sure footing and move forward with dignity. Decide today that your current life situation and challenges can and will change. Decide today that only what God says matters. He says you are His beloved. He says that you are the apple of His eye. Remember, you can do ALL things -even overcome mental health illness challenges. Press on to that high mark of experiencing your highest good. It's there waiting for you.

As you journey toward the high mark, remember you have people praying for you that you don't know about. Their prayers (and yours) are the pillar upon which you can stand. NO-thing that the enemy has presented to you can defeat you. Can any weapon formed against you prosper? "Survey says...no!" as Elder Doug Gould says.

Our loving, heavenly Father is the author and the finisher of your faith. He has every 'I' dotted and every 'T' crossed. And, don't worry, he has a limitless supply of whatever you need. Moreover, He delights in giving you exactly what you need when you need it.

If you've found yourself in these pages, know this…God loves you and He is a way maker. He heard me and gently and gracefully redirected my steps. If you ask, He'll hear you too and direct you to the proper people, places, and resources you need for whatever the challenge you face. In the words of Dr. Verlean Hailey Gould, "He loves you JUST that much!"

As a matter of fact, so do I.

Beverly Boyd

Beverly Ann Boyd, born and raised in Memphis Tenn., knew that she was a special child at a young age. She grew up with a Saved Sanctified Holy Ghost filled mother. Although her dad was not in the home, she knew and loved him. Sis Boyd was active in her local High School. She was on the cheer leading team and was known around the school. Although knowing the Lord she had a child at the young age of sixteen years old. Her mother was hurt but made her have her baby.

As years pressed on, she moved to California and married. During the marriage she struggled through many hard times but always remembered her relationship with the Lord. In an abusive marriage she rededicated her life back to the Lord. The Lord was her strength through all the tough times. She continued to raise her three children. While active in her local church she began to sing again. This gift had always been there, even as a child. Today her singing has blessed so many.

Her testimony is amazing. All that she has been through and she is still standing. She battled drug abuse, an abusive marriage, being raped as a child, and over 47 minor and major surgeries on her body. She would agree that if it had not been for the Lord on Her side, she would not have made it.

FOOTSTEPS

Beverly Anderson-Boyd

Have you ever felt like you were walking life's journey alone? I have had many of those days when I felt like no one was there with me, desperately wanting to be loved by anyone. Sometimes, I even questioned if God was there. As I became older, and wiser, I realized that God was there with me all the time. Through the ups, downs and uncertainties, He showered me with His unmerited favor and love. He delivered me out of some tight jams. Nobody but God could have done that. My life reminds me of the *Footprints in the Sand, Poem*: there were times I worried when I didn't feel or see his footprints but what a blessing to know that He was carrying me along the way.

I was born in Memphis, Tennessee on October 17, 1957, at John Gaston Hospital, a dark skinned baby who resembled her daddy's rich brown coloring. I wasn't the youngest child but I was the baby girl of the seven siblings. Named Beverly, my family nicknamed me Bell. I loved to sing and dance and was often asked to show off my talents.

I was born partly deaf and as time progressed I learned how to lip read. The ear, nose and throat specialist discovered the hearing problem: my eardrum was covered the way an alligator's ear is covered by skin. I had my first ear surgery at the same time I had my tonsils removed. I was three years old.

My mother was a caring, devoted, hardworking Christian woman. She was a 5'8" tall, light skinned, African American mixed with Cherokee Indian. One of the most memorable things about my mother was her beautiful smile. Her pearly white teeth and gold open-faced crown made her stand out like the gorgeous woman she was.

My father was a gospel recording artist who loved music. I'm sure my love for music came from him. He and his buddies would record on Fridays and Saturdays for the WDIA radio station. The station would broadcast on Sunday Mornings. I remember them recording on the big reel-to-reel recorders. Our home was filled with music which was a joy for me, the group, our family and friends.

In time, my parent's marriage started to fall apart piece-by-piece. My father started hanging out more with his buddies, most of whom were neither church goers nor filled with the Holy Spirit. He began to change into a different person. He started drinking and soon the abuse began. My mother stayed with him because of her children. She knew how hard it was to be a single parent. She had already experienced it. My father was her third husband. When they fought my sister and I would ball up in the bed, cover our heads with the blanket and cry. We didn't know what else to do.

There was one time my parents had a really big fight. My dad came home after hearing rumors about my mother being with another man. He grabbed her from behind and threw her on the bed. My mom fell to the floor. My dad took his foot and stepped in my mom's mouth. All I remembered was seeing blood everywhere. My mother's beautiful teeth were gone. My dad ran off. When my older brothers found out, they went to look for my dad. They were going to beat him up or should I say, beat him down.

My dad had more children outside of his marriage. He had started another family. I later found out that my mother knew but she didn't share it with anyone until one day my dad's sister, Auntie Tee Tee revealed it all. I didn't care about the affair. I just wanted my dad back at home. I was a daddy's girl. He loved me and I loved him.

After my parents finally separated, things got really hard. My mom struggled as a single mother trying to make ends meet. There were seven children living in the home at that time. She worked as a maid, waitress, and a nurse but no matter how busy she was she kept us in church.

My mom had a family friend named Mr. OC who would bring us food and help with the bills. I don't believe my mother had a romantic relationship with this man, but when things got hard, he would always be there. He even taught my sisters and I how to skate. When Mr. OC's wife passed away we began to see him a little more often. It was

160

great that he would help our family but no one knew that he was also molesting me.

I was six years old when he would pick me up from school and take me to his house. I always wondered why he didn't pick up my other sisters too. I knew they would get out of school a little later than me but I was the only one alone with him most of the time. His tactic was to play games and get me to laugh then the inappropriate touching would begin. He would put his big black hand on my leg and soon his hand would be under my dress. After it was over, he would give me money or ask if I wanted a toy. I felt so uncomfortable and uneasy around him but I never told my mother about it. I thought that if I told, he would stop helping our family. Years later, I found out that he was also molesting my other two sisters.

Being molested at such a young age, makes you think that something is wrong with you. There were times I've thought back over my life and wondered why certain incidents had to take place in my life. Was God there or did He disappear? Sometimes it takes a lifetime for God to reveal the answer.

On September 6, 1972, I was in the 10th grade. I was sick and got an early dismissal from school. All I wanted to do was get home as quickly as I could to lie down. Normally my mother would meet me but this time she couldn't. While walking home, I was approached by this strange looking guy. I remember seeing this guy standing in front of my house from time to time. He liked my sister but my sister never gave him the time of day. My mom would see him standing by our house also. She told us to watch out for him because he looked crazy. As I walked he came near me and pulled me close to him and made me go with him. He made sure I saw the gun he had in his pocket.

He held the gun to my side while we walked for blocks until we ended up in Lemoyne Garden Projects across town. He said, "If I can't have your sister, I'm going to have you." I was so nervous and scared. He took me into a house which I figured out belonged to his relatives. He tied me up and began to rape me, then his uncle raped me too. I was there for about four hours. I was numb and exhausted. All I could do was pray. I thought to myself, God you got to get me out of here. God heard my prayers. After begging and pleading, my abductor finally let me go but not without walking me half way back to where he met me. He told me that I better not tell anyone or he would kill me.

When I finally made it home, everyone had been looking for me for hours. By this time it was night fall and the street lights were on. As soon as I stepped in the door, I fainted. My family took me to the hospital. So many questions were asked. The police made me feel like it was my fault. Days later, I was so glad to hear that they found the rapist and arrested him.

I gave my life to the Lord at the age of fourteen. I loved Sunday school and singing in the choir. Sister Jones, my Sunday school teacher, taught me the Word of God. She made going to Sunday school fun.

By the time I turned fifteen years old, I was an outgoing enthusiastic cheerleader. I don't know what had gotten into me. I ended up getting pregnant by the star basketball player. I was so disappointed in myself. I felt like I let my mom, my family and my Sunday school teacher down. I couldn't sing in the choir or be up front anymore because my church didn't allow unmarried pregnant teenagers to prance around as if they approved. All my mother wanted was for all of her children to finish high school and receive a high school diploma. My goals were to finish high school and pursue a career in the Army. As a pregnant teen though, I thought my chances of completing high school were over.

I endured many restless nights and sleepless mornings, but I proudly finished high school with my classmates. I even attended my prom. I was grateful that even my teachers saw my efforts. One of my proudest moments was to walk across the stage and receive my diploma.

Although we were not together as a couple, my daughter's father would come and visit his child from time to time. His parents would not have it any other way. They didn't support what we had done but they made sure my daughter had what she needed. I received love from my daughter's father's baby sister. Although young, she would hang under me all the time. Annette became a great auntie to my daughter. Her love was shown in all that she did.

How could such a promising life turn for the worst? By the age of seventeen, I was very promiscuous and living the street life. I was an intelligent and nice looking girl and I was a prostitute selling my body and taking drugs. The Lorraine Hotel, the same Hotel where Martin Luther King was killed was my hanging spot. How in the world did I end up on the streets?

My mom and older brother would come and take me home but I would always find my way back in the street. I knew my mother was praying for me. She knew I was anointed by God to do great things but I was looking for love in all the wrong places. I found myself in the arms of different men wanting acceptance. I was exposed to things that no young woman should have seen. I was taken advantage of all while I was so-called-living.

While I was living on the streets doing whatever I wanted, my daughter was being taken care of by my mother. Finally, my mother was fed up. She said that she would not allow me to see my daughter anymore unless I got my act together. I loved my child but I didn't know how to stop what I was doing. The only thing I knew to do was to leave Memphis. I couldn't see a way out of my life style but to leave the state. I moved to California with an older cousin named ZD. My mom said, if I did well and got myself together, I would be able to move my daughter with me to California. I desperately wanted my baby.

A few months passed and I got a job and managed to get a place to stay. I was doing well. My mother didn't play. She meant what she said and stuck by it. Although my mom didn't believe that I was doing better, my cousin convinced her that I was. Thank goodness for my cousin encouraging me to get my life back on track. Getting my daughter back was one of the happiest days of my life.

By the age of twenty-one, I was married and pregnant with another child living in California. I stayed married for twenty-one years but seventeen of those years were filled with physical, verbal and emotional abuse. I must admit, there were some good times but it seemed to be more bad than good.

I would attend family functions with my husband and go to the movies, which was one of his favorite things to do, but my life had changed for the better. I was the type of wife and mother that always cooked, cleaned and made sure my children were well taken care of. Attending my children's school functions and sporting activities were a pleasure. Many times I didn't feel well in my body but I attended anyway while most of the time my husband stayed at home.

My husband always had a meal when he came home from work. As a matter of fact, I would serve him his plate first before anyone else. Soon we began to grow apart. He was in the military and was gone for long periods of time. There were times I had to manage the household alone all the while suffering through back surgery after back surgery. I longed for a healthy stable marriage. During this time, I had three children: two girls and one boy.

My husband felt like I was nothing. His persistent abuse really weighed heavy on me. No woman wants to be called out of her name and hit in front of their children. I hated for my husband to bring up my past and he would always bring it up whenever we had an argument about what I wasn't fulfilling in our marriage. I heard rumors of my husband cheating and soon found out the rumors were true.

As time progressed, I started using drugs again. I hid the pain and shame to cover up my feelings. It didn't satisfy me, it only brought me down. I went into rehab twice because it was hard for me to stay clean. I wanted so desperately to kick the habit but I couldn't. In the mist of my drug habit, God always showed me that he was there with me. I would be walking the streets and random people would say to me, "Why are you out here, you don't belong on these street." I even remember going to jail and the women inmates would say that it looked like I didn't belong there either. They knew there was something different about me. Before I was released, I found myself singing and witnessing to them.

My husband didn't understand that my life had changed and that I desperately needed God to lead and guide me. Things began to change after I truly dedicated my life to the Lord. I didn't go to clubs or drink any more and my husband would get mad because I went to church a lot. Church is where I received encouragement. I had grown closer to my church family and my relationship with God had grown tremendously.

After we separated, I lost everything. I stayed clean for six years and then relapsed. I finally went into rehab. It was time for me to put myself first. I couldn't kick the habit for anyone else but myself. I told God that if He was real, I was going to take Him at His Word. As of November 4, 2016, I have been clean for twelve years. This was a hard road but God displayed his willingness to stick by me through every temptation and trail.

Loneliness, pain and rejection can hunt you for the rest of your life if you allow it. Never allow people to cause you to feel unworthy. You are more than a conqueror through Christ Jesus. God is there with you walking beside you every step of the way. Never forget that. He is there through the good and the bad. I am a living witness.

God is married to the backslider. I have messed up so many times but God was right there with his loving arms wide open ready to accept me back. I have been sent to women like you, those who have never shared or talked about the abuse or the molestation. I will spend the rest of my life encouraging young women and men to not be afraid to share their pain with others. God knew you before you were born. You have purpose. You have to trust that God will carry you when you don't have the strength to carry yourself. Let the poem below remind you that you are never alone. God is always there. I love you, your sister, Beverly.

The Footsteps in the Sand

One night I dreamed a dream. I was walking along the beach with my Lord. Across the dark sky flashed scenes from my life. For each scene, I noticed two sets of footprints in the sand, one belonging to me and one to my Lord. When the last scene of my life shot before me I looked back at the footprints in the sand. There was only one set of footprints. I realized that this was at the lowest and saddest times of my life. This always bothered me and I questioned the Lord about my dilemma. "Lord, You told me when I decided to follow You, You would walk and talk with me all the way. But I'm aware that during the most troublesome times of my life there is only one set of footprints. I just don't understand why, when I need You most, You leave me. He whispered, "My precious child, I love you and will never leave you, never, ever, during your trials and testings. When you saw only one set of footprints, It was then that I carried you."

Sharon Norman

Sharon is originally from Georgia where she spent all of her childhood life. She moved to California in 1977 at the age of twenty. She is a single mother of two wonderful children. In the past years she has been involved in preaching the word of God, Pastor's aide committee, Care to Comfort Ministry, praise and worship team and children's ministry. She has also completed discipleship training courses.

Sharon has shared her testimony at a women's conference and different occasions throughout the years. What she enjoys most is sharing her testimony with individuals that want to come out of a gay lifestyle in hopes that they will be set free as she has been.

She has been blessed to be able to minister to people in different areas such as drug abuse, alcoholism and homosexuality. She stays blessed because God has delivered her in those areas. If you would like for her to speak at your women's conference or church she can be reached at Gbyfromsharon7@yahoo.com. She prays that someone is set free through her testimony. She wants everyone to remember never limit God by putting him in a box. May God continue to bless and heal you.

WHAT IS HIDING UNDER THE RAINBOW

by Sharon Norman

I was the fourth of eight children; six girls and two boys. We were raised in a small town in Southeast Georgia. My parents were what I would describe as typical southern parents. They were very strict disciplinarians that also believed that it took the entire neighborhood to raise children.

Attending church on a regular basis was a must, and to do what was right in the sight of God. There were times that we were in church all day; they even served lunch so we didn't have to go home. We were always surrounded by family and friends. We enjoyed family vacations to amusement parks in Florida. We traveled to Florida regularly to visit family and for shopping.

My mother worked as a housekeeper with a family that lived nearby. My mother was very soft spoken person but if she was pushed in a corner she would strike back especially when it came to her children. My father worked at the local paper mill in an area where he was the only African American in that position. My father had also become the only African American police in town. As a result we became a target of ridicule among our peers. My father was labeled an "Uncle Tom" among other African

Americans which meant he was considered to be excessively obedient and servile to the white man. People of our race perceived him to be complicit in the oppression of his own people. We all seemed like what some would call a typical family unit and we were but we all carried a secret. It was called not letting people in our business. That meant not to tell anyone what happens in our household. I now know that other families had the same problem but at the time it seemed as if we were alone in dealing with this issue. Dealing with our mother being beaten when we really didn't understand and it made us feel very helpless in every episode. When the abuse would begin I can, to this day, visualize exactly where we would stand during their fights. We all would gather in what was called the girls room which was right next to our parents room. We would stand by our closet in a circle putting our arms around each other's shoulders I called this the huddle— Crying out of fear and not knowing what was to happen next clinging to each other for comfort. Parents do not realize how this form of abuse affects their children.

As we grew older and began to swap stories about how we were raised, I found that there were some differences in each of our stories. One thing that was consistent was how we were disciplined and the abuse that was afflicted on our mother. If someone broke something and was afraid to own up to it, each of us would get a spanking for it in hopes that someone would confess and spare everyone else a spanking. If we acted out in school or told a lie we would get a spanking. We were never really sure what would start the fights between my Father and Mother. They would mainly be in their bedroom when the fights broke out. Each one of us battled our own demons, I believe as a result of being subjected to an abusive household.

I can remember the worst act of abuse came about when it affected us, the children. My father had been behaving strangely for a week or so, it seemed that he did not trust anyone. He would no longer give my mother money to take care of household needs like grocery shopping or other needs. This particular day he went to get groceries and he came home with rice and hamburger meat in various packages. My mother asked him where were the vegetables and they began to argue. He also brought packages of ground bones for the dog. I remember hearing my mother saying that he fed the dog better than he did his family.

I was in the kitchen getting ready to cook and my sister and brothers were in other parts of the house. I could hear my parents arguing and I remember saying in a playful voice to myself, if he hits my mom I am going to hit him in the head with the pot that I had in my hand. I began to walk through the kitchen to the dining area and I heard my oldest brother say to my father if you shoot mom you have to shoot me. I reached for the telephone on the wall and I thought to myself, I am calling the police on a police.

My father was in the process of getting ready to go on police duty with his service revolver. I remember a gunshot was fired above my head that went into the ceiling and at that point I did not remember what sequence of events took place. I think I went into shock at that point. There was a series of events that took place that I was told about by my brother. When I was able to get up I walked outside not realizing that I had been shot in my abdomen. I saw my neighbor beckoning for me to come to her but I was conditioned not to let people know what goes on in the house, so I returned to the house and started to lay on the sofa. At that point I realized that I was shot. I said to myself, if I am going to die I will lie on the sofa and die. My sister came from the back of the house and I noticed that both her legs around the knee caps were bloody. She began to try to look for my wound but by that time my father came in the living room and said come on let me take you to the hospital. We got in the car and he drove us to the hospital.

It was hard for me to breathe on the way to the hospital but my sister was there trying to comfort me. Once at the hospital, I began to yell for them to get my father out of the room. They began to cut my clothes off of me and I remember thinking that I had a brand new bra and panty set on and I did not want them to cut them off but they did.

This was a small hospital and they were not equipped to handle my wound there so I was taken to a larger hospital in Florida. I later found out that my mother was grazed on her forehead with a bullet, my sister was shot in both legs and my brother was shot in his arm twice. I remained in the hospital for two and a half months. My father was charged with four counts of what they called aggravated assault. He remained in jail about two to three weeks after I was released from the hospital. I do not know how he got out of serving time for what he did but he was released.

Most of my siblings experienced the abuse of drugs, alcohol and other problems as a result of having to deal with the abuse. I am not blaming our parents for all of our life challenges but I believe it played a role in them. We were predisposed to many things before we had the opportunity to make decisions on our own. I later found out that the way I felt about the opposite sex was a direct result of being exposed to my mother being abused. This is where the title of my story comes from. I hope my story resonates with others so that they may realize why they live the lifestyle of being gay.

At a very young age I knew that I had affection for the same sex. Yes, a Christian girl as myself harbored these feelings. I can remember being in the third or fourth grade having feelings for a girl the way a girl would feel about a boy. I did not understand the whole aspect of what I later found out to be called gay. I knew that feeling the way I did was considered to be a bad thing in the sight of God. Therefore, I hid my feelings for years in fear of being ostracized by others. So I secretly became an in-the-closet lesbian.

Being raised in a Christian environment, singing in the church choir and allowing the Holy Spirit to use me to dance before the Lord I had no reason to feel the way I did. Yes, I did have boyfriends and even got married because that is what was expected as a young lady. I also had two children a boy and a girl. The more I agreed in my mind about the way I felt the more prominent the feelings became. In my work environment there were two ladies that were gay and I confided in them the way I felt. They never passed judgment on me because I had a boyfriend and was not being true to my feelings. They also kept my secret to themselves because they felt that it was not up to them to out me.

When I reached forty years old I went back to college and in one of my classes I found myself sitting on the front row with other women whose sexual identity was also different. I now know this was a set-up from the enemy. The lady that was a lesbian began to show interest in me, eventually we began a relationship. At that time I was in a church where I was preaching, singing in the choir and teaching children's church. I was so afraid that my church family would find out about my lifestyle and I did not want any of the teenagers to one day see me out with a woman so I left the church.

I went to a church large enough that I would not be noticed and was not being held accountable for anything except me. As I tried to fit in the lesbian community I attended a lesbian support group. There I was able to express myself without being judged. I began to see a therapist that was also gay. She assisted me in dealing with my new identity as a lesbian. Because of my relationship with God I was never comfortable in a relationship with a woman. I would be okay with my lifestyle Monday thru Thursday but the closer it got to Sunday I could not do it. I would break up with her every week because for some reason I was delusional in thinking I had to get it right before Sunday. I later realized that a relationship with God is everyday not just on Sunday. My Christianity was always an issue in our relationship.

One day I attended a woman's conference and we broke off into different groups for separate discussions. When we came back together as one group there was one common thread from each group. Many ladies were dealing with homosexuality. Some stated that they had past relationships for various reasons. I felt compelled to expose myself because these were my sisters dealing with the same issue as me. The ministers asked every one that was dealing with that issue to come forward for prayer. I reluctantly moved out of my seat and went forward for prayer. They prayed for our complete deliverance from homosexuality.

When the prayer was over one of the ministers sat me down and said that it was good that I came up for prayer but why are you gay? That was one question I could not give her an answer as to why. I stayed out of a relationship for about four years without a problem.

During that time, I was a part of the pastor's aid committee and worked in the children's ministry. I felt like I was very giving to my church but one day I became sick and was unable to attend church and my church family did not call to check on me to see if I needed anything. I thought because I felt that I was an intricate part of the ministry someone would check on me and my family. My feelings were deeply hurt and I said, if my church family treated me like this I may as well go back to living the way I wanted to. So I decided to backslide; I went back into the gay lifestyle, I began to smoke weed and drink again. I felt like I was having fun doing all the things I use to do. I know it sounds like I wanted an excuse to go back to the things I use to do and maybe I did.

I did not tell my children about me being gay but during this time I thought it was time I told my daughter. When I told her she said to me that it did not matter to her who I was with and that she would love me anyway. I had placed a rainbow heart on my car and my neighbors kids knew what it meant so they told my son. He came to me as I lie in bed and ask me if it was true that I was gay and I had to tell him the truth. He asked me, "Mom why are you hurting me?" and those words burnt through my heart because the last thing I wanted was to hurt him. I also came out to my other family members. My mom did not say much but my father was very angry.

It was a three week period that I had backslid (I turned my back on my relationship with God) but it seemed longer than that. I was drinking and getting high almost every day. The spirit of depression began to creep in; at times I could not distinguish what was real and what was not. I was in a state of confusion. I did not realize that anger played a role in depression. When my girlfriend came over to spend the night we made her a bed on the sofa so the children would not be confused. She spent a lot of time with us. I admired the relationship she had with my children. For some reason I was not able to horse play with them and she did.

Everyone on the college campus knew that we were together as a couple. My therapist was very instrumental in helping me to embrace my sexuality. I was not very honest with her. My girlfriend at the time was aware of me seeing a therapist and she began to call her about problems between us. She stated that she listened to her but did not offcr any information. I did not think it was okay for her to entertain a conversation with her about me but she did. My therapist encouraged me to attend the local lesbian rap group.

I enjoyed being with a group of women with the same issues in common. We got together to go to clubs and parties, we also went to a few gay pride parades. I was so amazed at how many people there were in these parades and festivals. I said to God, "Lord there are so many of us here." They had a gospel stage at the festival and of course I went there. I met a young man that shared a story of how he was ran out of a church because he was gay. I really felt empathy for him because we should show the love of God not being judgmental towards others. We as a church need to show more compassion because most people do not know why they are living a gay lifestyle.

One morning I woke up around two o'clock in the morning and could not sleep so I decided to sit in my backyard. I rolled a blunt and fixed a drink and went outside and sat at my table. Before I could take a drink or smoke I felt the presence of God. It was strange because it was as if we were communicating Spirit to spirit. I did not speak any words but I asked him, "What are you doing here you see what I have before me." I felt very ashamed for God to see what I was about to do.

In a split second I began to see a vision of a little girl standing in front of a window. I recognize the window as the one in my bedroom. I saw the little girl's hair and it was in the three pigtails the way my mom use to fix my hair. I realized that the little girl was me. I knew my sisters and brothers were by the closet in a huddle crying and scared. My mom and dad were fighting in the room next door. I never knew that I separated myself from the huddle but at some point I did. I was not speaking audibly but I could hear what was being said within her heart. The child was talking to her mom from her heart. She was saying, "Mom, I am too small to help you now but when I get bigger I will help you. I will give you the things you need and I will love you the way you should be." I could feel the compassion this child had for her mother.

The vision left me with the understanding of where the affection for women came from. As I poured out my love for my mom the enemy twisted my thoughts to think that I had affection for all women. I also came out with the understanding of why I have dealt with depression. I held all my thoughts and feelings inside. One might think how can she get so much out of one vision but I cannot explain it. I do know that it was an act of God. I was so excited to finally know the reason why I felt the way I did. The question that the minister asked me months ago; I can now answer it.

From that point on I was unable to maintain a lesbian relationship. I had begun to attend another church where the pastor knew about my relationship. He showed me compassion and helped at the same time through some rough parts of my life. If he was not the type of pastor that believed in winning souls I may have been lost. He did let me know that he did not want to carryon conversation with me concerning my relationship and I respected that. The Lord spoke to me and said this church is where I was sending you. That is why the enemy was throwing all his fiery darts at you.

In the three weeks of backsliding I went through a lot and it actually seemed longer than that. I continued to battle other issues but not about being gay. I have shared my testimony at many events in the hopes that my story will resonate with someone and bring them back to a true relationship with God. I can truly say that God has delivered me. If this is your story I admonish you to trust God for a change and He will show you "WHAT IS HIDING UNDER THE RAINBOW."

Rhonda Culton

Rhonda Culton, commonly known in her community as "Mrs. Rhonda," is characterized for her boldness when it comes to the work of God. Many are touched by her real, relevant, and raw uncompromising message of the Gospel. She captivates many by her energizing message of hope. She believes that no matter what comes or goes, people can make it with God on their side.

Rhonda's enormous love for people is heart-felt by those led her way. Her positive attitude has drawn countless people into the body of Christ. Her energetic style of praise and worship has challenged many to take their praise to another level and her ultimate desire is to see people *delivered* and *set-free* from the bondage of the enemy.

Rhonda has participated in two book compilation projects entitled *Un-Stuck*—a book that shares the stories of women from across the country that have moved beyond setbacks and burst into victory, and the *Un-stuck Workbook,* —a workbook designed to help women in ministry. She is co-author of a devotional book called, *Women on the Vine,* which describes the importance of the connection we all should have to the Vine, which is Jesus Christ.

Rhonda released a book and workbook entitled, *What to Do While Waiting on Boaz*—a reader and applicable workbook designed for the single woman waiting on her spouse. In November 2013, God blessed her to release *Called to be Your Own Boss* and *Document It.--a daily documentation book for teachers.* Recently she Co-Authored a book entitled, *How to Get Your Book Published Fast* and more books are in the making.

Rhonda is the CEO of her own daycare consulting business where she helps those locally and regionally with creating an effective and efficient childcare center. Additionally, she works part-time as a Child Development Professor at local community colleges and as a California Early Childhood Director Mentor. She holds a Bachelor of Arts Degree in Child Development and a Master of Arts

Degree in Human Development. She works diligently alongside her husband, Pastor Fabian Culton, who is the Founder of Most Holy Place Community Church in Lake Elsinore, California. Together, they are the proud parents of three beautiful children, Maelina, Marquis and Malerie and grandparents of two boys.

She is committed to the vision of pointing people toward God and will do all that is necessary to ensure that the vision is carried out. Connect with Rhonda on Facebook and Instagram @rhondaculton, on Twitter @Ladyculton, and on the web atwww.thechildcareconsultant.com or MHPCC.net. Email Rhonda at rhonda.culton@yahoo.com.